What People are Saying about The Rise and Fall of Psychic Medium

This book is absolutely great and I love it, it will be so relatable to other Spiritualists! As a working Medium, I can totally resonate with the stories of the churches, circles and Nicky's clear explanations of reincarnation and those taken too soon. This book is pure testament to how Nicky can go on working so wonderfully well despite her health. Everyone from developing Mediums to people who are curious about the afterlife will love this book especially as it is written by such an accomplished Medium.

Ronnie Buckingham – Psychic Medium and Bestselling Author of *Medium Rare*

This is a gem of a book and a truly valuable contribution to spiritual literature. Nicky opens up the mysterious world of the Psychic Medium to us, and gives us the answers to so many of the questions we all have about the meaning of life, the afterlife, God and angels. It really is all here! It is a book that is certainly needed at this time! It confirms that there is no division between the various energy vibration levels - they all inter-mingle, inter-merge and inter-connect. Our loved ones who have passed back to Spirit before us are only a thought away, still looking after us, still helping us and still guiding us!

Thank you, Nicky, for a marvelous, soul-uplifting book!

Eileen McCourt - Reiki Grand Master Teacher; Spiritual Author and Tutor.

I love Nicky, she's so real and full of life and laughter. This book is a great representation of Nicky as a person and an extremely gifted Psychic Medium. It illustrates beautifully, why the Spirit World has chosen her to represent them as a trusted storyteller and conduit between the esoteric realms and the Earth plain.

She has been entrusted with sacred knowledge and shares this with the kind of integrity and grace that I would be honoured to trust my spirit loved ones' souls to communicate with. Nicky represents compassion and respect in her tales of truth on her journey of *The Rise and Fall of Britain's Best Medium* and if I was to be appraising her employ with her *bosses*, the references would be nothing other than glowing.

I love Nicky. She is real, she's strong, she's honest and so hilariously funny.

Annie Lloyd – Reiki Master, Holistic and Pellowah Practitioner and Teacher

What another great book by the amazing Nicky Alan who details her journey from being a Police Detective investigating murders to a point where she was one of the top celebrity Psychic Mediums in the UK.

The story is told with her usual touch, where her sense of humour and personality shine through so they are not just words on paper, it's like she is actually reading the book directly to you.

Not only is this an interesting journey, but I also really think the evidence she gives in this book will help people who are grieving for their loved ones. This will help them see that we never die we just 'move on' and that one day we will see them again.

As a nation of animal lovers there is even a chapter about our pets, their souls and the afterlife.

Great job - can't wait to read her next book.

Lindsey Cox – Retired Police Detective - Animal Reiki Practitioner

The Rise and Fall of Britain's Best Psychic Medium

Nicky Alan

Copyright © 2022 by Nicky Alan

All rights reserved. No part of this book may be used or reproduced by any means, graphic, electronic, or mechanical, including photocopying, recording, taping, or by any information storage retrieval system, without the written permission of the publisher except in the case of brief quotations embodied in critical articles and reviews.

Contents

Prologue 1

Chapter 1: The Haunting 3

Chapter 2: Circles 7

Chapter 3: The Calling 16

Chapter 4: The Popping of My Cherry 23

Chapter 5: The Churches 30

Chapter 6: The Plights of Platform Mediumship 38

Chapter 7: The Pleasures of Platform Mediumship 49

Chapter 8: The Miracles that Spirits Bring 60

Chapter 9: From The Mouths of Babes 71

Chapter 10: The Esoteric Cord 81

Chapter 11: Murder Most Horrid 86

Chapter 12: We Also Save Lives 96

Chapter 13: We Can See Your Future 111

Chapter 14: We Wanted to Go Home 121

Chapter 15: We Will Seek You Out 131

Chapter 16: When Two Become One 143

Chapter 17: Spirit Guide Upgrades 152

Chapter 18: Pet Heaven 164

Chapter 19: We Are Not Dead Yet!..173

Chapter 20: Now for the Angels! 180

Chapter 21: Is Anybody There? 189

Chapter 22: Seeking Out a Medium..206

Chapter 23: The Rise to Celebrity 215

Chapter 24: The Fall from Celebrity 223

Chapter 25: What My Bosses Taught Me 229

Dedication

This one is for you mum. I did it again! X

Acknowledgements

There is no way on this earth plain that I could have created this book without the stars of the show, the Spirit people! Their diligence, humour, patience and sageness has enriched my life and helped me to reach millions of people all over the planet. Top job afterlife peeps! Thanks for never giving up on me.

Thanks to the legend Medium that is Ronnie Buckingham for his endorsement, Eileen McCourt one of my most favourite authors and Lindsey my poor mate who is always stuck with reading my stuff and saying what she thinks! Annie, I should be endorsing your book as your words are always so eloquent. Anna, yet again at the eleventh hour your message pushed me to believe in this book.

Finally, Denver Murphy, my editor, my counsellor and my Yoda of everything booky and wordy! (He will so want to change that sentence!). Thank you for being there throughout the whole journey and being the best at what you do. Your gracious energy that went above and beyond during my tears, fears and triumphs was exemplary. Here's to the next one…if you'll have me. x

Prologue

★ ★ ★

When people think of Mediums it can go two ways. Some think we are magical people who have a very special gift whereas others do not believe a single word coming out of our mouths and perceive us to be preying on vulnerable people. Basically, the Sceptics versus the Believers. This little journey of mine is not to prove anything to the non-believers as I wouldn't waste any of my energy on them. I feel that sceptics believe that once you die, that's it, just a dark void of nothingness and that makes me feel sad, so I will leave them with their lonely and hopeless view of their future! This morsel of happiness, humility, laughter, tears and wonderment is meant for the people who have an open mind or know that there is an afterlife. Perhaps it could even convert the dark void people when they read some of the gobsmacking tales I have to share with you.

I won't name and shame anyone and it goes without saying that I will preserve the identities of all Spirit people and clients. I have therefore changed some of the names to protect their privacy.

Either way I am going to let you in on a whole new world of how Mediums and Psychics work. I will bring you some pretty amazing tales of spirit contact and how they have proved time and time again they are still alive, just devoid of their physical body (that I refer to rather unpoetically as their meat suit. You will learn that I really do say it as I mean it, a spade is a spade and all that…).

Spirit people thrive, they do not change up there in Heaven, they don't suddenly appropriate a harp and start floating on a fluffy white cloud. They stay real and true to who they were down here, scoundrel or saint. So, you will witness a lot of humour in this book and why not? We cannot all sit maudlin and mourning our loved ones under a black cloud for the rest of our lives. The world needs a bit of hope and happiness and most of all laughter, so I hope you smile more than you cry during this journey of mine. Spirit people love to let us know they are there looking over us and will jump to any Medium they can find if it means getting a message to their loved ones down here.

I am a fourth generation Medium and if you haven't read my first book (then why not? Joking) you will not know that I have been psychic since birth and so is most of my family, particularly my dad's side. I was an Essex Police Officer for eighteen years; a majority of that time as a Police Detective ultimately investigating Major Crime. I used my gift a lot in the police, (some anecdotes to follow!) but was medically retired from an injury on duty and before I knew it, and after a couple of dicey jobs, I was forced into becoming a full time Medium.

In fact, that is exactly where I will start; right at the beginning of my professional *talking to the dead* journey. It began in my bedroom.

CHAPTER 1

The Haunting

———— ★★★ ————

'Nicky!'

'Nicky!'

I was laying there in the dark and feeling that familiar tingle down my spine, my scalp alive with the fizzing energy of when Spirit people are nearby. It felt like I was dipping my head in freezing lemonade. I couldn't deny the bloody voice whispering my name urgently in the darkness.

'Nicky!' To be fair I was a bit concerned, because for the first time I had no clue who the discarnate voice calling my name belonged to. I was used to my nan, my dad, my mum and my grandad coming for a visit, (they are dead by the way) but this was a whole new kettle of fish. I didn't know this woman at all.

'Nicky!'

Oh, for God's sake, there was no point in ignoring it, 'What? What do you want?'

'Nicky!'

This went on for about five minutes.

I tried everything: 'Go to the light, go back home, bless you for coming now please go back to spirit —'

'Will you just fuck off!'

I jumped out of my skin, my partner at the time, Ryan, could also hear the voice! He didn't worry about the grace of spirit contact, he had to get up early and all he could hear was someone calling Nicky!

It worked though; the voice stopped calling. I felt so guilty that Ryan had sworn at a spirit person. I was trying love and light and he just smashed it with the F bomb!

'Could you hear that as well?' I asked.

'Yes, I could, you need to sort out what that's all about, Nick.'

He was not impressed and I was none the wiser.

It's fair to say that this continued night after night. No matter how polite I was the voice carried on. Then it was joined by other people calling my name in my bedroom.

I had been medically retired from the police service two years before. I was gutted, I am not going to lie. I was discarded and the punch in my heart knowing I was no longer going to be there to help put bad people away gnawed at me like a malignant cancer. I was now teaching teenagers at Southend University on how to prepare for emergency service careers and hated every minute of it. I was going through a breakdown and thought I was basically projecting my energy or even hallucinating, both of which could be ruled out now that Ryan was hearing the voices as well. So why was I suddenly getting an entourage of dead people in my bedroom at night? They started walking up and down the room, stamping, shuffling, talking away - it was a bloody nightmare!

It reminded me of the scene in the film *Ghost* where Patrick Swayze sang in Whoopi Goldberg's bedroom, *Bottles of beer* and

Henry the 8th! They kept annoying me every night and it didn't stop there. Don't get me wrong I had been doing readings since I was 21 years old, 14 years previously. Back then, I would be a police officer during the day and at night I would be going to people's houses hosting psychic parties. I wasn't exactly a *spirit virgin*, yet they had never plagued me like this before. The last spirit person that I had seen in my house was a one off, Ryan's brother, who had just hung himself. It wasn't pleasant but at least he had come to say goodbye, bless him. So, to have this kind of paranormal stuff was unheard of, especially when they were all strangers!

Another day I was ironing in my lounge, (believe me that is a miracle in itself!) when Ryan said, 'Nick, look up.'

Above my head, the huge black gothic iron chandelier was swinging rather eerily from side to side. It wasn't as if a breeze had just whooshed in because it then rose up towards the ceiling, stopping and before going even higher, swung back again.

'What the hell is going on Nick? This house is alive!'

I couldn't answer him. To be honest, I had no clue what was happening. If I walked past a light, it would either flash, dim or explode. Everywhere I went I heard my name being called, no longer just at night. I honestly thought I was losing my mind, but I knew that I couldn't be as Ryan was hearing and seeing a lot of what went on. The doorbell would ring and there was never anybody there. It was nonstop and getting worse. I am open-minded to everything that I witness and certainly do not put everything down to the Spirt World, but this was without a doubt totally paranormal.

The thing that really sent me to another layer of despair was when the baby started. It was the sound of a new-born screaming at the top of its lungs. At the best of times, not something you would want to listen to for any great length, so when this started, I was really getting the hump. It sounded like it was in the next room but when I got up and checked, the noise would move to the stairs. I would then follow it but never manage to catch it. I made sure none of my neighbours had newly born babies, nope no arrivals near me at all. Night after night the baby came and on top of my depression from being retired and lack of sleep and the fact that I had to get up to work in my new job, I was starting to get close to the edge. What did they want from me for God's sake? Why was I being incessantly hounded by Spirit people?

It didn't take too long to find out why I was being relentlessly visited by dead people. To be honest it was a relief as I was picturing myself being sucked into a telly if it continued! Wow what a journey I was about to embark on because when it all became clear, I realised that my life would never be the same again.

New. Beginnings.

CHAPTER 2

Circles

——— ★ ★ ★ ———

Now, I need to zoom you back two years before my spooky visitations, as that's really where it all began.

I was at home and had just received my letter telling me that I had been medically retired from the police. I felt numb as I took my cup of tea onto my patio with the rest of the mail. It was a beautifully sunny summer's day, with cornflower blue skies, a blistering sun for that time of year, but with a refreshing breeze. I sat in my garden staring up at the sky, looking for some sort of 'Eureka' moment that would help me shape my new life and find a new career.

A strong burst of wind then whirled through the garden and the local newspaper blew off the table and onto my lap. It had opened at a page that was advertising an Evening of Mediumship for the following day at a local hall. I had never attended one of these events before as I saw them as watching what I could already do from birth. Something fuelled me to go, though.

The following night I went to the hall and, as soon as I walked in, it was clear the place was heaving. I quickly dropped into a seat and felt unusually anxious as I waited for the two Mediums to venture up on stage. We were alerted that the demonstration would start in five minutes. I started to look around the hall. To the left of me it was lined with windows along the whole length of the room. I was about to look away when my eyes caught the reflection of a man. He was about 5'9, with a rotund build, bald head and aged somewhere in his sixties. I remember thinking that he should sit down soon as the show was about to begin. I looked to my right to see where he was standing, as he was obviously being reflected in the window. There was no one standing up, everyone was seated. Confused, I then returned to the supposed-reflection and, to my surprise, he was there waving at me. I looked at the people sitting next to me to see if he was waving at them. But no, he nodded at me and waved again!

In my mind I then heard, 'My name is Ron, I was a taxi driver.'

'Was?' I thought. I realised with a jolt that this man was a spirit person. As the understanding descended over me, he was then joined by another, younger, man. Dressed in bike leathers, he had black short hair, was slim framed and looked to be in his twenties. They were both solid forms like any other human being.

'I'm Mark,' he piped up. 'I died on my bike.'

They then just stood there smiling at me.

I sat there mesmerised by them, completely oblivious of everything and everyone else in the room. I had never seen Spirit people for that amount of time in full manifestation. They were normally fleeting visons or strong 'third-eye' visions where you see their form in your mind's eye. I stared at them and they just stared right back at me.

'Yes, you!' I heard in the room.

The person to my right nudged me and I jumped in my chair. I felt a little silly as the whole audience was looking at me. I looked up to the stage and saw that one of the Mediums was staring right at me.

'Can I talk to you?'

'Yes, yes of course!' I managed to stammer, being completely aware of the two spirit men still watching me.

The Medium said that he had my dad with him and told me he could see Koi Carp swimming in a pond. I smiled at the fond memory of my dad and me sitting at a pond, watching Koi Carp at the hospital when my sister was being born. I knew it was him as he told Mediums this every time he connected.

The Medium went on to say I had endured a big shock because of the recent change in my life and that I had to dust myself down. He said that I had to get ready as my life was going to go into full speed. I would be known all over the world for what I did and that I would be teaching and writing and prove exceptionally successful.

I smiled and said *thank you* but had absolutely no idea what he meant. How would people know me all around the world, I was an ex-Detective? He made it clear though that my life would change immensely and, with the evidence he gave proving my dad was talking, I had to wonder what the hell was going to happen.

At the end of the evening the two men were still there looking at me and smiling. I thought, *it's now or never.*

So, I got up, took a breath and approached the female Medium without even thinking. She was either going to believe I was a nutter or a wannabe when I told her about the two people in the window.

As I described the men and said their names, her jaw dropped open. I had described her stepson and late father-in-law.

She was so impressed that she told me to come to her circle that she ran every Monday night at a local hall. Now, I had been around tarot cards, tea leaf readings and all sorts of spooky stuff growing up with psychic family members but had never really attended any classes or development circles.

Circles have been around for donkey's years; they were especially popular during the Victorian era when physical Mediumship circles were all the rage. Physical circles are where physical phenomena takes place and either objects are being moved or ectoplasm emanates from the Medium. There were totally false Mediums who faked everything but then you had the real deal such as Helen Duncan, one of my heroines.

There are two types: open and closed Circles. Open Circles are ones that anyone can attend whenever they want whereas closed ones are usually held at people's houses and are a lot stricter. You have to be there every week and devote your energy and time to the Circle without fail. You usually practice links to the Spirit World, participate in joint meditations and all sorts of psychic exercises to further your abilities.

I turned up the following Monday and, to my surprise, saw that the hall was full to the rafters. I felt quite excited as I would be sharing my time with likeminded people. The evening was a disaster, though - the problem I found was that I was too advanced despite not ever sitting in a Circle. So, when people were bringing in feathers, gold balls of light and butterflies, I was bringing in dead relatives, one after the other. Rather than encouraging me and appreciating my potential, the Medium came across as almost jealous. She kept putting me down and made me feel like I was showing off. I wasn't showing off at all, I was merely doing what she asked by going into meditation and repeating what I saw!

I attended the following week's session but felt isolated, vulnerable and, once more, like everyone was looking at me with contempt because I was finding it all so easy. I was a naturally advanced Medium attending a beginner's circle class. No one wanted to help, no one liked the fact that I had better abilities than the teaching Medium.

Needless to say, I never went back there again! However, if you are an ambassador for the Spirit World, having a connection to the divine is like a drug, you keep getting pushed to link to them. You just can't lose the urge to want to join them, commune with them and pass on their messages.

I found another circle with a Medium who did a lot of work in the spiritualist churches. When I saw a spirit person enter the room and mentioned it, she promptly screamed, stood up and ordered me to tell it to go away! What the Hell? It's no surprise I never went back there either!

I had got talking to a lady who ran a new-age stall in Rayleigh market a few weeks later. She stated that she would get me invited to a closed circle. I was excited about this as a closed circle was perhaps what I needed - a group of more experienced Mediums who would welcome me at my advanced stage.

In a few weeks I got a call to say I would be welcome to attend the closed circle. I was so excited!

I turned up with the anticipation churning my belly. There were six ladies present, all of them a lot older and, I thought, wiser.

They introduced themselves and said the circle leader would use the first twenty minutes to conduct some soul recovery. Now, I am a bit of a sceptic when it comes to this soul recovery malarkey.

It's just my opinion rather than a case of wrong nor right. I just can't see how a Medium can visit all over the world and gather up lost souls and take them to the light. I had always been told by my granddad that it needed to be pretty much face-to-face for someone to be able to cross over. Anyway, we all held hands and the circle leader closed her eyes. She started to sway and let out a long moan.

'Oh, for God's sake!' I thought, as she then started to writhe and claim that she was bringing over two thousand Christian soldiers from some war a few hundred years ago. I even saw her open an eye to check we were all looking at her! It was laughable. All the other circle members were willing her to gather every Christian soldier she could, as she moaned and groaned her way through this apparent miraculous recovery.

I was nearly weeing myself with hysteria and so desperate to laugh that I had to take my hands away from the other people to cover my mouth, hoping to disguise any utterance as a cough. A couple of the 'Mediums' glared at me for breaking the link in the circle. (To me that's a load of tosh as well. Breaking the circle, why? What is going to happen?)

Oh Jesus, Mary and the wee donkey, what a load of shite! As I sat there pretty unimpressed and disappointed, especially following my initial excitement to be invited, I jumped upon hearing a voice.

I recognised it as my dad, Alan.

'Pick up a pen and paper!'

In my head I said, 'Did you just talk to me?'

'Yes!' he replied. 'This is a load of old shit, let me show you something,'

I grabbed a pen and a bit of paper from a table next to the circle.

'Right, close your eyes, let go. Keep your pen on the paper and watch what happens.'

I did exactly what my dad said.

Before I knew it, I was coming round and everyone was staring at me.

I looked down and realised that I had written a whole page with my eyes closed. I now know it to be *automatic writing*.

The writing was in French. I couldn't believe it.

I had six sets of eyes regarding me with disgust for not fully supporting the writhing rescue of those poor lost Christian soldiers! I had also channelled something amazing and they knew it.

Let us just leave it that I never returned to that circle either!

I later heard that they were bad mouthing me saying I was full of myself and was just a show off. It hurt a lot. I was learning very quickly that the 'spiritual' circuit was bitchier and more backstabbing than the police!

The most amazing thing was I translated that bit of paper. I had channelled someone called Louis Claud de Saint-Martin, who was recounting the Battle of Dettingen in France. He said that he was born in 1743 and, having gone through the rigours of war, left the army to practise spiritualism. He then went on to talk about how he raised the awareness of spiritualism in France. Google is such a brilliant tool for confirming the spirit contact you get! I could not believe what I was reading. The fact that I had channelled this information and had written it in French whilst my eyes were shut, only then to find out it was all historically correct, was just mind blowing!

My dad had shown me that I had an amazing gift and that, yet again, I was wasting my time in this circle.

These two experiences really put me off finding another circle if I'm honest. Having been treated badly, along with the fact that I'm extremely sensitive, I ignored the endless twinges of wanting to connect with the Spirit World and got on with jobs that I had absolutely no passion for.

Two years followed before it finally happened, so let us whizz right back to my hauntings. After a few weeks of my house being alive and housing a screaming baby, I was about to discover what the madness was all about!

My friend Debbie phoned and said that she was going to see a Medium but the friend who was meant to be accompanying her had cancelled. She asked if I would go instead as she was a little nervous. I agreed as I thought I might, if I was lucky, get an answer to the craziness that was happening in my house. The Spirit people had now upped their game to shouting my name loudly in addition to the screaming baby, making me sit up in bed, heart palpitating and screaming, 'What do you want?' with no immediate answer.

The Medium stared right at me as soon as Deb and I approached her front door. Without a beat she said, 'The baby won't stop crying until you start to work for the Spirit World full time. They will not leave you until you serve Spirit, it is your destiny.'

There was nothing I could say or do. I stood there rooted to the spot until she dragged me into her house with a huge show of impatience. This is when everything turned on its axis and I was never going to see my life in the same way again.

Holy. Shit!

CHAPTER 3

The Calling

―――― ★ ――――

That Medium was called Aggie. She was Irish, had a wicked twinkle in her eye and was the best circle leader that I've ever had.

She ushered us into her lounge and, to my embarrassment completely, ignored Deb.

'You opened your mouth. You upset the wrong people,' she said to me. 'You had a back that was damaged so badly and now they have thrown you away like yesterday's newspaper. This has all happened for a reason - you have to serve spirit now, that is what you were destined to do. The day you surrender, everything will stop in your house.'

I couldn't believe what Aggie was saying. I had not so much as uttered a word since she had opened the door, but she was completely spot on! I had been medically retired with a back injury and, as soon as the decision had been made, I never heard from the police again. It was like I had died and, even now, I know a part of me had melted away to an unseen darkness.

She then said she had to do Deb's reading. Leaving the lounge, I walked through what felt like huge thick cobwebs. I was spitting and rubbing my face.

'Don't be such an eejit!' she said. 'That's ectoplasm from Spirit. You can't wipe it off!'

I looked back a little shakily and waited in the kitchen for her to finish with Deb. After Deb's reading she pounced on me and demanded to know when I was going to start in her closed circle. Her fiery blue-green eyes sparkled with a flash of challenge. I gave in and told her I would be there the following Monday.

Monday came all too quickly and, to be honest, I had mixed emotions. I didn't want to look like a complete idiot and get anything wrong but, by the same token, I didn't want to do what I had been doing and bring Spirit people in, only to be met with jealousy. As I turned up on the night, I was greeted by a beautiful older lady who welcomed me in with such a loving smile. The rest of the circle members were equally friendly and immediately I felt at home. That's what any novice Medium should feel like, at home, comfortable in their own skin and confident enough to express everything that they experience during the circle session. If you can't tick these boxes, budding Mediums, move on to the next circle until it feels right.

After introductions were made, we were asked to go into a meditation and focus on any Spirit people that came near to us. Previously I had sat back and waited for them to come in, but this time I asked in my mind: 'Come to me if you want to communicate with anyone in the circle.'

Straight away and with absolute precision, a man came into my mind's eye. He moved closer and closer until I could see every line on his face. He was an older generation man as he sported an old fashion moustache and presented as if he was in a black and white photograph which I now know represents someone not of this time. His features were so clear it was unbelievable. I had learned that when I see someone in black and white, they come from older generations rather than recent or modern times. He then showed himself standing with his arms around a beautiful lady and said the name Anne.

When we opened our eyes, I felt an emotion that I had never experienced before as I blended with this man. Pure love was coming from this man. I think it was because I felt so safe and secure in this new circle that I was able to experience it.

As I started to describe him, I then realised that the lady who welcomed me in on the doorstep was called Anne, and we were sitting in her house. Her eyes glistened with love and nostalgia as I described her husband to a tee. She got up silently and went to a side drawer to pull out a photograph. I gasped as I looked at it. It was the exact same image that he had shown me in his mind. I was gobsmacked. I remember thinking: 'This shit is real!'

The next week, Aggie stared right into my eyes when we had come out of our group meditation. She stated that she had seen one of my Spirit Guides around me.

'His name is Hammerhawk and he is a Native American, an absolutely gorgeous man with the greenest eyes and he is your healing guide.'

I must admit, I took this with a pinch of salt as every bugger who is a Medium tends to have a Native American guide!

It wasn't until the following weekend that I really should have grabbed that salt and thrown it over my left shoulder.

I had booked a few days at what I call Hogwarts. It is actually named the Arthur Findley College. It is a centre for psychic studies, development and all sorts of spiritual pursuits. It is a huge manor house, set on the most stunning grounds nestled in a little bit of countryside next to Stanstead Airport in Essex.

Again, another apprehensive move as I thought I may be going to some sort of cult centre or a mass gathering of tree huggers. I needn't have worried. Despite the obvious cliques there between staff and regular students, I found it both pleasant and rewarding to be around like-minded people who understood me. I was surprised to see people from Europe, Canada and the United States attending this unique place.

Overall, it was a bit pricey, and so one of the cheaper options was to share a room with two other people. I found myself there with another girl from Essex and this exotic beauty from Sweden. Now, this Swedish dish had a habit of doing Yoga poses in her thong and frankly nothing else every morning before breakfast. It wasn't the largest of rooms so you couldn't really avoid her lithe limbs doing their thing.

I used to want to kidnap her and force-feed her lard as I watched her tanned torso, devoid of anything close to fat, go through its stunning ritual each day. One morning I had only just sat up in bed when she stood over me, pert breasts swinging just a wee bit too close to my face, and said, 'I have something for you.'

It had me thinking that we were going to be entering into a really awkward lesbian moment! I heaved a sigh of relief when she handed me a scroll of paper.

'This is your guide; he came to me last night so I drew him. His name is Hammerhawk.'

I couldn't believe what I was hearing. Hammerhawk! That's exactly what Aggie had said! I opened the scroll and, to my amazement, this strong handsome, green-eyed Native American, sporting a red-tipped feather on his headband, stood aloft with a hammer in hand. Her perfect scrawl (as sickeningly perfect as her body!) wrote *Hammerhawk your guide heals you* at the bottom of the page.

For some reason I felt emotional. This was one of my first true synchronicities that I had witnessed as a Medium, the first of thousands to come. I thanked her unreservedly and thought nothing of hugging her half-naked body!

That day we were doing something called trance dance, in a class where we would sway to enchanting music and ask for our guides to come close. Hammerhawk came along with my soul totem animal, a wolf. My guide introduced himself as Khan, saying that was his family name whilst his tribal name was Hammerhawk. He showed me so many amazing things, including the previous life we had together. This is from when he had chosen to be my healing guide. He would not only bring me soul healing when I needed it but he would also assist in any healing I gave out. My connection to him was instant, along with an infinite love I can't describe.

Most people who are developing cannot wait to identify and connect with their guides, so I was chuffed that I had not only seen and felt him, but he had given me the most amazing synchronicity to prove who he was.

Two days later I was in a psychic development class. Here we had to blend with the person in front of us and provide information about them with no spirit contact. I got really frustrated as I could not blend with anyone in front of me on a psychic vibration, all I could see were the dead people standing next to them. I even embarrassed myself by bursting into tears and leaving the class when the person in front of me responded 'no' to every observation I made of them. I went up to my room and said out loud: 'For God's sake, how am I going to do this if you don't bloody help me blend with human energy?'

Well, later that afternoon in meditation a gorgeous lady with long raven, silken hair came to me. She was adorned in a long black cloak with a large hood cascading around her milky skin - her eyes large and soulful. She was standing on a cliff and holding out her hand. In it were a number of runes which she blew on, turning them into white doves that flew into the sky.

She said, 'I am Catherine and I am now giving you the gift of prophecy.'

For people in the UK, she looked like the woman in the Scottish Widow adverts. She had a Celtic vibe and I adored her on sight. After this meditation, I could see auras clearly and could feel ailments in people and what was going on 'inside' them. I couldn't believe it.

I arrived home from Hogwarts feeling like a top spiritual guru! I had learned a lot about disciplining myself and understanding how to blend with Guides and Spirit people alike. Most unbelievably of all, the Spirit World had twice corroborated in no uncertain terms one of my guides in the most amazing way. To then get introduced to a second one was beyond my expectations.

The same thing happened with my soul guide Julianus. He came and introduced himself and the synchronicities kept on coming from him time and time again. He convinced my sceptical mind that he was real (especially when showing me our past life in

Rome) and that he and the other two had a vested interest in guiding me through this quirky tapestry of existence we call life!

Details on my three guides are in my other book, *M.E Myself and I: Diary of a Psychic* (shameful plug!) but all three stand by me even now - they are always close and never allow me to feel alone, ever.

The next time I attended Aggie's circle, (which I loved even more once we started going for a curry and a bottle of wine afterwards!) I felt exceptionally confident and safe in demonstrating my abilities. Three of my friends in the circle even picked up on the name Catherine!

I shouldn't have felt so confident, though, as within weeks Aggie dropped the death bomb sentence: 'You are ready to do platform. Next week you are coming with me to do a public demonstration.'

Oh. Pants!

CHAPTER 4

The Popping of My Cherry

―― ★ ★ ★ ――

It was a boiling hot summer's evening, so I already had sweat running down my back and thighs before I even got out of the car. The nerves made it even worse. I could feel my underwear soaked with nervous sweat and the heat of the evening. All of my friends from the circle had turned up to support my debut fledgling demonstration of Mediumship at a spiritualist centre in Grays, Essex.

I was close to pooing my pants as we entered into the hall, with well over a hundred people waiting expectantly for their dead relatives to rock up and make them feel better. I feigned a smile, hoping it would hide my terror as I was introduced to the church organisers. I was then whisked away to a quiet room where Mediums go to prepare. Far better there than where people were staring me up and down as the fresh meat in the Medium circuit.

This happens at all such evenings, where the Medium is provided with a private space so they can 'link up' in peace away from the crowd and prepare themselves for spirit contact. This is where you do your visualisations and prayers to show you are available to work. The Spirit World can then see your bright light and your guides will start to draw Spirit people near to you. Well, that's how it's supposed to work. I didn't and still don't care about that bit - as long as they are there to communicate when I need them, I am a happy bunny!

My prayer was along the lines of: 'For the love of God, don't make me look like a twat! If you have passed over and your loved one is in the audience, get here now!' Not very spiritual, I grant you, but it was all I could come up with at the time. When we were called onto the stage, I felt like a condemned woman being dragged to the guillotine. I was beyond terrified.

I could not believe that Aggie thought that I was good enough to stand in front of these paying guests and bring them their loved ones in a professional manner. I had only been in the circle for a matter of weeks but had to trust her experience and judgement. Before I knew it, Aggie had done a few links and I was being ushered onto the stage as a Fledgling Medium. That's what the churches call you when you are a novice, a Fledgling. I just kept picturing a baby bird spreading its wings on the edge of a nest and then plummeting to the floor in a big, huge splat.

My imagination even went one further because as I stood on the stage alone, I pictured a dog pooing with its legs shaking. Mine were hardly holding me up as I was so scared. I remember thinking, *No pooing dog, no pooing dog!*

Aggie proudly introduced me, saying that I was an amazing conduit between the earth and the Spirit World and no doubt would bring some lovely messages to the audience. *NO PRESSURE NICK!* For fuck's sake!

I couldn't run, even though the side door was enticingly open. I couldn't stand there mute, so I thought *sod it*, it's now or never. I can't remember for the life of me what I even said when I started talking. Some pants about being happy to be there and how much I loved spirit and felt so privileged to be a Medium.

The crowd just looked at me as if to say, *Shut up and get on with it, I want my mum!* You could see they were seeking to pass judgement from both the look in their eyes and their body language. *Is she any good? Will she bring me my dad? Should I have gone to bingo tonight instead?* Bearing in mind I was a youthful looking 33 and had a really common gob, they most probably thought she is too young and too inexperienced to be the real deal. However, some were smiling and willing me to do well, especially my circle friends. So, a mixed bag really.

I took a breath, gulped some water down and shut up. The seconds ticked by like eons of time as I waited for some sort of vision, feeling or thought that I could identify as not belonging to me. I had already in the car on the way there done a visualisation where I opened my head (Crown and Third Eye chakra) and imagined a big ray of light shooting up to the sky. That was my way of saying to the Spirit World that I was ready to work.

Then, it happened.

Thank Christ!

I saw a man on a motorbike and unfortunately, I saw him ride it off a bridge. I then observed a pub called *The Royal Oak* and him going in to see a blond guy. He was smiling and, as I looked at his companion, I saw the names Gary and Jeff in my mind.

Gary was then crying his eyes out. This was a suicide; I could feel it. Don't ask me how I knew, I just knew he was going into this pub to say goodbye to Gary before speeding off to plummet from the bridge. This was not an accident.

I relayed exactly what I saw to the audience. I was met with nothing but silence. I repeated what I had seen and felt. Nothing. I swear I heard a church bell offering a toll of doom and in my head tumbleweed was rolling along a dusty road. FOCUS NICK!

Oh shit! I started to panic - this was not going well. Was I just making this up in my head? Was there really a spirit person communicating with me? I started to search the audience, desperate for a recipient for my dead person. My first lesson with hindsight, I wasn't trusting the spirit person or the process.

Those before me keenest to judge looked like the cat that had got the cream. Their Cheshire smiles echoed their inner thoughts, *Knew it, she's crap!*

I suddenly realised that I had forgotten to mention the names I had seen, so I said pleadingly: 'Sorry, I forgot to mention that this man who took himself over said the names Gary and Jeff...'

Straight away a woman raised her hand and said, 'I think you might be with me.'

PRAISE THE LORD!

'Oh okay, so you understand the name Gary then?'

'Yes, that's my husband's name, but I'm not sure...'

'Okay,' I swear it was like drawing teeth! 'Who is Jeff?'

'It was the name of his friend that died.'

At what point did you not understand this message at the beginning? I am thinking, desperate to not let this frustration etch itself all over my sweating face. It is not as if a lot of people drive off a bloody bridge!

'And the Royal Oak pub?'

The sceptical *she's too young* bunch suddenly started to sit up.

'My husband drinks in the Royal Oak pub.'

Yep, I definitely had the judgey ones paying attention now!

'Okay,' I said through gritted teeth. Why the hell didn't she put her hand up straight away? 'So, you do understand everything I have said then?'

'Well, yes, Jeff was my husband's best friend. Jeff came into the pub and had a drink with Gary. He then left and the next thing we knew the police told us that he had driven off a nearby bridge. He had left a note at his house. It broke Gary's heart and the guilt has never left him.'

BOOM!

Get in! I wanted to throttle her for being so bloody stupid and allowing me to stand there like a plum for five minutes but, my God, the rush I got from knowing I had the right recipient was overwhelming. I learned from that day that the whooshing feeling is a huge adrenaline hit from the spirit person in acknowledgement of me successfully receiving what they are trying to convey. It is like a sneeze amplified a thousand times, where your whole body tingles and fizzes. It's an amazing feeling. To be there on your own and relying completely on a spirit person to bring you information that just one person will understand in an audience was pretty much short of a miracle. I was actually relaying information from someone that had died and this lady could understand everything that came out of my mouth. Elation would be an understatement.

I continued to bring this woman fact after fact to amazed gasps of delight from the audience. Jeff did an amazing job of conveying how sorry he was, that he hated every minute being on the earth and pleaded for Gary to feel no more guilt as he would never have been able to stop him from taking his own life. I cannot remember any of the other readings I provided that night but this, as my first on stage, will be imprinted on my heart until I go back home to the Spirit World. The rest were just a blur.

After the dem (that's what us spirit workers call a public show) I received rapturous applause. Some people even stood up! I was booked in my own right to do a full dem alone by the organisers. I couldn't believe it, but it did come at a hefty price. Jealousy can be a cruel mistress, but more of that later.

After working, Mediums are always on a high because they have been blending with the pure and light energy of Spirit people. I was buzzing!

'I knew you could fecking do it!' smiled Aggie proudly as the circle gang and I went to a local pub where I ate a huge meal and drank a bottle of wine. This is normal, apparently. Most Mediums feed themselves to get grounded and ease the come down with a cheeky glass of vino. Who knew? More bonuses every minute! I can see why because when you are 'back on the earth' you can feel a little depressed and heavy. It is almost like your soul has had a taste of home and now has to be human again! To be honest, I think that many Mediums have addictions and the vino thing is just an excuse. I did notice their propensity to be overweight, smoke liked chimney and/or drink heavily. Perhaps when we weren't buzzing on the vibrations of a spirit person, earth life was just too flat for us to cope without some kind of substitute.

All I knew was that the high was second to none and I wanted more of it. You always got a little tingle from doing one-to-one readings, but the power of spirit visitation at a dem was intoxicating and I wanted more. This had been my 'breaking in' night, my cherry had been popped! With my humour and confidence in public speaking, I knew that I was going to skyrocket in the Medium circuit. It felt good.

I learned a lot in those few weeks.

One is to never doubt a spirit person and know that a lot of recipients in an audience become completely devoid of any ability to recollect anything when they are getting a reading (me included).

Two, I was not only Clairvoyant (Seeing) but I was Claircognizant (Knowing) and Clairsentient (Feeling) as well. That was rare. (Little did I know that I would be able to smell and taste what spirit wanted me to as well in a matter of months! That was rarer than unicorn poo!) The concept that all of my senses could be used by Spirit people was unimaginable!

Three, I now knew my guides and felt like a proper Medium!

Four, I had also started doing private one-to-one readings at my friend Claire's salon in Rayleigh and the first night I returned home, the spirit baby stopped crying and my house became as quiet as a mouse! I took that as an, *at last we have you working for us*. The powers that be had won.

Cheeky. Minxes!

CHAPTER 5

The Churches

★ ★ ★

The day following after my debut dem I was like a woman possessed. I scoured newspapers and websites looking for the next service or dem in any spiritualist church or centre within travelling distance. I went to every dem that I could in between doing readings at the salon, so that I could watch the Mediums and learn the trade. Some of the Mediums were pitiful and I mean pit-i-ful! Their delivery, lack of empathy and general inability to blend with spirit was shocking, but then there are always bad apples in every walk of life. Some of them were magnificent, so I watched them wherever they turned up, learning from their presence and delivery of messages to the crowd.

One in particular, was a man called Bill Rich. He was a stocky East-End man with no airs and graces but the wisdom and knowledge that he imparted on people was mesmerising and top class.

I remember going to a psychic fayre near Danbury and Bill was headlining the event. He brought my dad through during the dem. The evidence was superb and I had no doubt whatsoever that he was talking to my father. He delivered the messages with humour, humility and accuracy. I had my first Medium man-crush!

I do not know what possessed me to approach him, but I did. He was due to go to a centre in Corringham to do a dem the following week. The centre was run by Fred and Dierdre, a darling couple (now in the Spirit World) who were dedicated to healing, developing Mediums and promoting the afterlife with their lovely centre. I so desperately wanted to get up in front of the congregation there so I thought sod it, just ask him!

I explained to Bill (Like a bumbling buffoon) that I had just recently done a dem at the Grays centre and would love to do another one.

He smiled, his eyes lit up and he said, 'I heard about you! By all accounts you did a lovely job there. You are in Aggie's circle from the Rayleigh church, aren't you?'

OMG! Bill Rich had heard about my night! Jesus, news travels fast!

'Yes,' I replied. Not much else I could say, to be fair. 'I heard that you are doing Corringham next week…'

'Darlin' come up there and I will let you do a couple of links during my dem.'

I was so happy, I whooped with joy and gave him a hug,

'Thank you Bill, I will never forget this.' I whispered.

I haven't either! I recently saw Bill; he came to do a dem at a local spiritualist centre in Devon. It was amazing to meet up after so many years. He still delivers his messages in true legendary style, like the Yoda or Gandalf of Mediumship! One of the first things he said as he mentioned me to the crowd was: 'This is the girl who I let do a couple of links for me at a dem in Corringham and then bang, she was everywhere!'

I love that man! He will do anything to help a fellow Medium reach their potential and, believe me, there aren't a lot of them around, especially when you get really well-known.

With this newfound confidence, the following day I went to a church in Southend. I watched the dem and the Medium was pretty mediocre; coming across as patronising and cocky which were all useful learning points for me. I must admit I kept thinking to myself that I could do so much better. Afterwards, I spotted a lady who I thought was one of the committee members. I decided to take a chance and ask if I could be considered for doing a service.

The conversation pretty much went like this:

'Hi, my name is Nicky, sorry to bother you. I recently did a dem in Grays and it was well received and I just wondered if I could be given a chance to do a couple of links—'

The biggest mistake I made was to approach this cow bag in front of a lot of people.

'Sorry, you are who?' she interrupted loudly, crinkling her nose up like I was a freshly laid bad smell.

I cleared my throat and started to feel the unease snake through me.

'Sorry, my name is Nicky, I'm a Medium—'

'Oh, you are a Medium! Why didn't you say! Ha-ha!' She then looked back at her cronies, encouraging them to smirk with her.

Had I just entered a church that's supposed to be full of love or a bitch from hell room full of sarcasm, with this being the queen?

'Well, yes, I am a Medium.' Don't go red Nick, stop your chin from trembling. I have to add at this time the old copper in me was long gone. Sensitivity is par for the course when you're a Medium, meaning you can find yourself crying at anything.

The whole group had gone quiet and were just watching me - no doubt waiting for her to take the piss even more.

'Dear, you have to be training in a circle for at least ten years, have you done that?'

'No.'

'No, I didn't think so (another smirk). We don't accept novices here. You have to train - you can't just come here and do a service'

'I'm not a novice, I'm kind of advanced but—'

'Oh, you are advanced, are you?' She said louder than needed, dripping in sarcasm. 'Where have you worked then? How long have you been doing it for? How come I have never heard of you?'

The room stood silent as the cronies started to shift a little uncomfortably. She had pushed it WAY too far.

'It's okay, sorry.' I then stumbled out of the church and promptly burst into tears. Love and Light, I thought, was the order of the day with spiritual people. How wrong was I! I had a big wakeup call coming!

What a bitch! She didn't put me off going to churches to study my trade, but I didn't say boo to a goose at any of them. I was just waiting for my evening with Bill.

Little did that evil woman know, karma was going to bite her on the arse. Don't ever try and cross a spiritual ambassador who is on a destined path to serve the Spirit World!

Some of the churches I found to be like going to a funeral: dull and dismal. They were very God-like, and full of prayers and hymns. The churches themselves were damp and smelled like wee and stale cake.

Not that God is a bad thing, I just have my God, which I have seen and been in the presence of. My God is an Omnipresent, pulsating core of light, energy and power that can connect to every single person and living being in the Universe. As I see it, there is no God that would create rules for us to follow and sins that gain his wrath. My God just wants us all as one intelligence spreading nothing but love, humility, spiritual wellbeing and divine knowledge handed down from our ancestors. There is no book to abide by, no sins to torture yourself with when committed, and no prayers that will keep you safe from the boogie man. He just wants your immortal soul to experience life reincarnations and learn from them in between a sublime eternal existence with your soul family.

Anyway, I'm back off my soapbox! Other churches were vibrant and trendy, offering healing, readings, workshops, open circles, stalls full of spooky dookie stuff and trips away to spiritual locations. The people in them were welcoming and kind and would answer anything that you had to ask. It was an eye-opener and enabled me to go to the churches that I preferred which, needless to say, were the trendy ones devoid of too many prayers, hymns and old people dribbling and snoring in the front row.

The evening with Bill at Corringham was amazing. This kind and generous man with no ego, got up and stood by my side as I tentatively introduced myself. There was a huge crowd of about seventy people who were all so warm and supportive. Despite my legs doing the pooing dog thing again, I delivered three beautiful messages to the congregation. I noticed halfway through the first message Bill sat down. He knew that I was okay and totally focused.

One was from a lady, Jill who had passed over with breast cancer. Her sister, Leanne, was in the audience and the spirit girl gave one bit of evidence that I call the 'golden nugget'. You can say as much as you like to a recipient, but they always have something in the back of their mind that if it's mentioned you have nailed it and proved beyond any doubt that you are talking to their dead loved one. This of all things was Jemima Puddle-Duck from the famed stories of Beatrix Potter! I could see it in my mind so clearly and knew that it was important, so I mentioned it. Leanne sat with her jaw gaping and initially couldn't say anything apart from: 'How did you know that?'

Erm, because I am talking to your dead sister? I thought in wonderment.

'Because your sister is laughing about it and told me to mention it.'

Basically, Leanne had bought Jill a Jemima Puddle-Duck shaped planter for Christmas. The following year Jill had given it back to her as a present, having forgotten who it had come from! Although Leanne said she was miffed to begin with, it ended up a longstanding joke on how tight her Jill was! Jemima now stands on Jill's grave with pride. That, my friends, is known as a golden nugget moment. It is great to have funny moments like this, as it raises the vibration of the crowd. I want to celebrate the Spirit people, not have everyone feeling depressed and down, crying or, even worse, bored. After the dem, Fred and Dierdre asked to book me in my own right. I couldn't believe it!

Following that evening the church circuit became alive with this new kid on the block called Nicky. Nicky was the name on every spiritual jungle drum. I had come from nowhere and was now all over the place. I was getting phone calls several times a day to be booked. I ended up serving over eighty churches throughout the UK. My waiting list for one-to-one readings hit six months.

It appeared that when the Spirit World want you as an employee, they will create every opportunity to get you out there. It was only in a few months' time that I would be approached by a Hollywood TV producer. But let us not get ahead of ourselves, as I want to regale you with some pretty interesting stories as a newbie church platform Medium!

I do need to end this chapter on a really juicy note, though.

One of those several calls from the churches made me want to literally dance around in my garden naked doing a ritual victory dance!

It went a bit like this:

'Oh hello, is that Nicky?'

'Yes, how can I help?'

'I do the bookings at (I really can't divulge the church, sorry!) in Southend. We got your number from Fred and Dierdre and would love for you to come along and do our divine service on a Sunday?'

Now, let me tell you, Divine Service on a Sunday is the holy grail of church Mediumship. Sunday Service is reserved for the veterans and the high-profile Mediums. They were asking me to do a Sunday as my first gig! I was ecstatic!

'Oh, that would be lovely, thank you so much,' I said enthusiastically.

When the lady laughed on the end of the phone, it sounded familiar. 'No, thank you! Oh, that is great, we will be so honoured to have you here as we have heard amazing things about you!'

OMG! It pinged in my head; it was THE BITCH! Oh, how glorious karma was and oh how I looked forward to that Divine Service, it was only a couple of months away…

Happy. Days!

CHAPTER 6

The Plights of Platform Mediumship

———— ★ ★ ★ ————

As with my book, *M.E Myself and I*, I would not be able to remember most of my adventures if it wasn't for my soul journal. It pretty much has my whole life documented in it. Some of the tales I am about to share are so memorable I would never forget them, whereas others come from delving back into my old journals.

The church circuit provided the most valuable experiences I could ever wish for. I learned how to do a proper spiritualist church prayer and address. An address is basically a spiritually inspirational speech, delivered to the congregation before you crack on with the messages. I learned which churches to loyally support and those to avoid like the plague. I also learned that the Mediums in the church circuit could prove amazing friends or brutal rivals. There were quite a few of them who had their nose put out of joint because I had come from nowhere and was taking the spiritualist church movement by storm. I would hear on the grapevine snipes that people had made and comments that I was too big for my boots. It hurt me a lot and eventually led to me working on my own and not taking many offers of joint Mediumship evenings.

I did notice that I was changing as the months went by. Being an open conduit for the Spirit World had its problems. I was becoming more sensitive by the minute. I would cry at literally everything and thought I was going down into a depressive episode quite regularly. Bearing in mind the things I saw as a police officer that needed me to be strong, this new way of being was quite alien feeling vulnerable and emotional most of the time. I discovered that I was starving after a dem so would eat like a neanderthal to get my energy back and to ground me. The body doesn't work very well with light continually coming through from celestial layers. It has a dense energy in order to walk around the earth plain, so the two had to be perpetually balanced.

The biggest lesson I received was that there was no way on this earth you could sustain a living from church work. Most of the churches paid around a fiver for a Medium to do a Service. I remember one that cost me a fortune in fuel for the three hour round-journey getting there. After the service, the old lady gave me a chocolate cake for my efforts that day. I was gutted as they were taking £4 on the door and the place was heaving. A learning curve on which I realised the need to confirm how much you want to get paid before you attend!

Most of the church people were lovely and covered your petrol, but that was about it. I didn't care, though, as what I was learning was far more valuable than money. However, one place in London made me think, *you really are taking the piss, love.*

It was wintertime and it took me two hours to get to this place. It was raining cats and dogs, making the journey difficult and tiring. Remember what I said about the damp churches that are like entering into a funeral? This was one of them. As I walked in, the energy literally felt like someone had just died a minute ago. The lady that ran the place was as miserable as sin and for the first ten minutes completely ignored me, pretending to be busy with the hymn books. I wanted to turn and go back home, but then I thought

I am serving Spirit and the people, rather than this rude old bint! The congregation started to shuffle in and I literally mean shuffle! I was finding it hard to see who was dead and who was alive, they all had such a look of misery etched on their faces as they plonked down on their seats. I noted that the entry fee was £3, there were eventually about thirty people in the audience, so they took £90 on the door for a short evening service. Not one of that congregation was under sixty.

Mediums are as good as their audience. We have to work in a high vibrational energy, it helps feed the link between the Spirit World, the Medium and the recipient. That night it was like wading through treacle. There was no energy whatsoever. A man in the front row even proceeded to go to sleep as soon as he sat down. The only energy emanating from him was the odd isolated fart and a snore that made him wake up, only to nod off again within seconds. I felt totally disillusioned and hated every minute of it. Every spirit communicator tried their best to get their messages across but, by falling on a lifeless energy, much got lost in translation.

At the end of the evening, I breathed a huge sigh of relief. I thought at the end: *I have travelled for two hours to get here, so do not accept £5 for this shitty night!*

'Is £5 ok, dear?' the old bint asked.

Say no Nicky, say no!

'Yes… oh um, actually, would you mind if it was ten, please? It's only because it's a four-hour round journey and—'

Her tut interrupted my plea for more pennies. She then made me jump as she shouted: 'Pete!' whilst staring at me like I had just killed her puppy. She was absolutely enraged that I had asked for ten pounds!

It was hilarious looking back, but at the time I only found delight in envisaging me strangling the life out of her. She had Pete bring over a bag of coins. I am talking 5p, 10p and 20p pieces. She then proceeded to count out - very slowly - the amount, in between looking at me with such venom that would have given me five seconds to live if she could have manifested it into actual poison! I wasn't going to back down. The slow counting of every silver coin made me more determined to stay put, and I didn't give a shit if it took an hour.

Eventually she gave me a carrier bag full of the coins (despite me seeing notes of various denominations go in the entry box and the raffle!) and said very bluntly: 'There you go, ten pounds.' Seriously, it was like I had robbed her! I was so pissed off driving home in the pouring rain. The journey took me three hours because of roadworks. Unbelievably that lady told others I was too expensive and greedy! (As I have already said, the church jungle drums are swift and efficient!) Thank the Heavens I never had to return there again. What with it being during my 'people pleasing' and 'being so grateful that I could work as a Medium' stage, I would have said *yes* if she had asked me back!

Another hellish night was when a Medium called me up (I will never forgive her) and said she was feeling ill, asking if I would take her night at a centre. Little ol' *I will turn up for the opening of an envelope* me said *yes* straight away. It didn't take long for me to see why she had pulled a sicky.

It was another London venue, so another two-hour drive into the city. I was pretty run down too, with the most horrendous cystitis. I doubted my Satnav when it started to take me into the loins of hell on an estate where there were burnt out cars and gangs of youths standing on the corners. *No,* I thought as I put the central locking on. *This definitely can't be right.* But oh yes, it was. The centre was like a meeting room under a block of high-rise flats, a mix between a working man's club and a bingo hall. I got out of the car after trying to park it as closely as possible to the church, stupidly thinking the Spirit World would protect it as I was on a spiritual crusade. Frankly, it was a dump. I walked into the foyer and all I could smell was stale booze and cigarettes. It was disgusting.

The hall held about 150 people. I noted here they had paid £7 to get in and there was a huge queue at the bar where harsh faced women were buying pints of stout. I was shitting myself. Not because I had to do a dem, because the people looked like they would slit my throat if I got it wrong! I steeled myself and bounced in as happy and bubbly Nicky, only to be met by looks of disdain and *who the fuck are you* on most people's faces.

I kept trying to find out who was running this tip of a place, but I was ignored by everyone, leaving me stood there like a prize idiot. That familiar feeling of humiliation and a need to cry started to threaten its presence. I walked to the toilet (blinking cystitis!) where there was an old lady with no teeth smoking a roll up whilst sitting in a cubicle with no door. It wasn't the most comfortable of conversations in the world but she did direct me to the organiser. It turned out she was the one serving the pints! I approached the bar, introduced myself and tentatively tried to ask if people could stop smoking during the dem but was met with a snort by the organiser.

Hardly surprising considering she had a fag hanging out of her mouth. The bar was also open during the demonstration so I had to shout above the general humdrum of people packing as much alcohol into their bellies as possible!

At most centres and churches, you have a person to chair the meeting. They introduce you, generally run the evening and time you. I had no one to chair, all I got was fag lady saying, 'Right you're up.' That was it! When I stood in front of the congregation, they looked me up and down like I had five heads and tentacles for legs. I did not feel welcome. I started my introduction choking through the blue haze of cigarette fumes, when a lady in the front row let out a loud yawn which made everyone laugh. This was not going well.

The first two links I gave out to the audience were not taken. The more the silence grew the more the people started to fidget and whisper. I was sinking fast. The tears threatened to come. 'Please spirit help me, you put me here, now deliver!' I begged in my head.

'Come on Nicky, don't you dare let them beat you, get on and do what you are supposed to do. You were right on those first two poor people who wanted to come through. Believe in yourself.'

I jumped as I became aware of my beautiful nan Eva standing right next me. I was in such shock! I could then smell her; a mix between moth balls and talcum powder. This was when I first gained Clairalience - I could now smell spirit.

I was so excited to know that she was standing there with me against this motley bunch. Emboldening me, I cleared the last spirit person and waited for the next one. They kind of queue to my right and I let them come into my energy one at a time, unless there are people that are relations or friends who want to come through with the original spirit communicator. They sometimes jump the queue but, typically, and especially after all of my practice, they behave themselves. Refusing to say another word usually did the trick for any would-be queue jumpers and they learned to wait their turn. Some were clever though; they would try and hoodwink me so they could have more time with their loved ones! They would come through aged around the time they died and deliver their message. Then after a couple of links they would arrive back twenty years younger, pretending to be a different spirit person. It was hilarious and exceptionally human on their part!

With my nan stood next to me, comforting me, I saw her bring an elderly lady in. I could see the name Elizabeth and Jean. I then saw the word TWIN. I looked at an elderly lady in the front row and just knew I was with her. Sometimes the Spirit people told me where to look, or simply said the name of the person they wanted to talk to. On other occasions I had to throw it out to the audience to find out where I was.

'I think I am with you my love,' I said as I looked at the lady. 'Do you understand the name Elizabeth and Jean?'

'Oh,' she said, smiling at her neighbour, 'I am Jean!'

Thank God! 'Okay, so I am with you then?'

Us Mediums always use this term being 'with' someone. It generally translates as, 'I have a Spirit person here and I suspect they want to communicate with you.' When the sitter says, 'Yes, you are with me,' they are stating, 'Yes that sounds like my spirit loved one.'

'Possibly.'

WTF? 'Oh, okay, do you not understand the name Elizabeth?'

'Who, Betty? Yes, that's my sister's name.'

'So, I am with you?'

'Not sure dear.'

'Is she your twin?'

'Yes, she is. Our Betty!'

'Right,' I am trying to laugh and help warm up the audience but, nope, you could still hear a pin drop.

'So, I think it's safe to say I am with you then as I have your sister here from the Spirit World?'

'No, I don't think so.' I could have dive bombed her! She looked confused and I had no idea why. I continued for another five minutes, with her understanding everything I told her and yet denying I was with her!

Eventually I said, 'I am not being funny Jean, but you understand everything I am saying about your sister and so I must be communicating with her. Why am I not with you then?'

'Well, you can't be talking to her because she is dead, dear.'

This caused everyone to explode with laughter but somehow, I thought it was at my expense. Despite the frustration, it was a good learning experience. The lady had honestly thought I was a fortune teller and that I couldn't be talking to her sister as she was dead. Bless her heart.

'I'm so sorry!' Betty communicated to me. 'She has a bit of dementia and just doesn't understand the process. Thanks for trying!' Poor Betty just wanted to talk to her little sister. I watched her disappear from my mind's eye and then saw nothing again. I stood up straight and smiled through gritted teeth. The natives were getting restless. I told my nan that, unless I got a solid link next, I was going to walk straight out of there.

She did not disappoint.

I watched a young boy with dark hair around 14 years old being murdered. Behind him was the name of the road he died in.

'I have Alex here. He was stabbed by gang members and I know that he passed away in Victoria Street. He wants to talk to his mum who is in the audience. He is saying that the court case was bad and the boys didn't get enough time in prison as it couldn't be proved which one did the actual stabbing.'

I pursed my lips and waited in silence.

Shortly after a lady at the back screamed: 'Oh my God yes, yes! That's my Alex!'

It turned out the whole family were there. They cried and they laughed as Alex proved very cheeky and made some very naughty comments about his family members and friends. They gasped as he communicated to them where he was and who he was with. Best of all was when he informed them that his murderer was already back in prison for life and that they should all move on and heal, knowing that justice had been served.

As a Medium you can sense peace with the spirit person. They have crossed oceans of frequencies to get to this particular space and time to commune with their loved ones. It really is miraculous. What is also very odd is that, despite me being poorly, when you are linked up your own personal body and feelings take a step back. You feel nothing apart from what the spirit person permits you, which I found to be a bonus when I was in slight pain or simply tired. That is why I can't remember readings as they are not my thoughts, words, or feelings - they come from the spirit person completely. It used to get embarrassing when people asked if I remembered talking to their dad or brother. Most of the time, and unless it was extraordinary, I couldn't remember a thing! Thank goodness for my trusty journal!

In that moment, watching this emotional family smile and hug each other, all of the frustrations, the rudeness of human beings and the place I was in, dissipated as I saw the true beauty of what had just taken place. This poor boy had brought evidence of his survival and peace to his whole family. And I was the one in the middle enabling it. I felt glorious and truly humbled. After that reading the energy of the room rippled like a Mexican wave. Everyone sat up and finally wanted to engage. I carried on, knowing my duty was to the Spirit World and with the improved atmosphere I smashed one accurate reading after another.

At the end I got a huge round of applause. Yet the organiser hardly acknowledged me as she got up and started shouting about a handbag being stolen during the demonstration! You couldn't make it up! She then walked over to me and slapped £15 into my hand, a sharp contrast to the solid grand she must have taken on the door, never mind the huge profits from the bar. I felt a little sick as I left. It was beyond me how such a rude person could be in charge of a 'spiritual' centre.

The Medium who had set me up to do this made me feel upset and exposed. In fact, on the way home I cried and came close to throwing it all in. I had been taken advantage of by both the Medium and the centre. One was not amused! The only good thing that came out of it was that my car hadn't been wrecked whilst parked outside!

Us Mediums have a bloody tough job, so think about that when you next go to see one. We know that you will listen to every word we say and take it to heart, so the pressure on us is immense. We are desperate to get it right for you, so cut us some slack! Also, church centres, think about a fair amount to give us Mediums when we are travelling through hell and highwater to get to you! This includes donation only churches - attendees should put in more than 2p! I am not joking; I have seen people toss in copper coins and yet can afford to smoke as they leave the dem.

Driving home I also reflected upon the cardinal rule that I had broken. Don't work when you are feeling poorly - it diminishes the energy and the quality of the link. My cystitis was burning away and proceeded to get worse day after day.

I must say at this juncture that these are just a few nightmare scenarios to give you a taste of the reality behind the scenes of a working Medium. Believe me when I say most centres were absolutely beautiful, with kind and loving people running them and attending them. So let us look to the lighter times I experienced in those early days in the next chapter, plus I cannot wait to tell you about *the bitch*!

Love. Karma!

CHAPTER 7

The Pleasures of Platform Mediumship

———— ★ ★ ★ ————

I adored my days working on platform where the experiences were out of this world, literally! My bubbly and confident approach to speaking in public helped me win over most audiences. To hear their squeals of delight and their gasps when I produced a 'golden nugget' was delicious! I also hold particular fondness for the laughter that was had during my church visits. In a lot of them, I had to put my best face on and act as if butter wouldn't melt. I used to be a roughty toughty copper and I have a penchant for being a bit of a potty mouth, so I really had to watch my language!

The church that I was going to on this fine day was in Kent. I had never been there before but I knew it was potentially going to be a wee and stale cake job. After the service or dem, you usually get tea and biscuits and, if you are lucky, some homemade cake. On particular occasions it was akin to doing an *I'm a Celebrity* eating trial, as you munched through a rock-hard sponge, but their hearts were in the right place. If you were early, you would also get the same privilege in the quiet room before the dem. The room in Kent prior to the dem had church volunteers in as well, so I couldn't link up alone. It was indeed a wee and stale cake place but the ladies were wonderful and kind. A rather (ok, very!) large lady came huffing and puffing towards me to bring me some biscuits and a cuppa. I accepted the goodies with grace and then watched as she walked over to a chair. The chair was very narrow and had certainly seen better days. You did not have to be psychic to predict what happened next! The lady lowered herself whilst smiling at me and, before anyone could blink, the chair exploded beneath her weight and down she went falling on her back, her legs akimbo displaying pantaloon-status knickers. Oh, my good God, I snorted tea from my nose as everyone fussed around her whilst she rocked on her back like a helpless tortoise. I offered to help to which one of the rose-faced ladies exclaimed: 'No dear! You are the Medium! You must prepare yourself!' As if I was some demigod. It was hilarious. As if I could prepare myself in the current climate anyway!

I was biting down on my cheek to stop the laughter as I didn't want to appear unspiritual. At one point two ladies tried to pull the hefty woman up. One of them grabbed her arm and as she was pulled up, she let out the loudest fart. That was it, I was finished - I ran to the toilets and literally wet myself laughing. It was one of those moments that, as soon as you revisit the scene in your mind, it brings the hilarity and gut-aching laughter back to the fore. I had a wet crotch and started to panic as I was supposed to go up on the podium. I just didn't know what to do!

Eventually I gained some sort of composure and learned that a couple of gallant men from the congregation had helped the poor lady up. I went onto the stage with toilet paper stuffed in my knickers. I was desperately trying to maintain a serious and spiritual façade but all I kept seeing in my mind was a flailing woman and a farting old girl! I had to think of beginning with a joke so I could let out some of the laughter. It was hell trying to stay focused. Thank the lord it was a 'churchy' service so I only had twenty minutes dem time. I laughed for pretty much the rest of the day. They were all happy with the service so no harm done!

I used to go to a darling church in the East End of London run by a very witty and dry woman, Jackie. She took no nonsense from anyone and was a devout spiritualist. This place was an SNU church (Spiritualist National Union) and so had the prayers. hymns and whatnot but I didn't mind as she was such a joy to work for. The congregation were a bit hit and miss. There was the standard snoring, dribbling man but it wasn't too much of a distraction. The more practice I got at these churches the more I was learning to ride the energy, be it good or bad. I noticed a family come into the back row just as I was walking up to the podium. There were about nine of them and they appeared to be composted of the great grandma down to the great grandchildren, so all generations were present and complete. They were obviously desperate to communicate with someone as they all looked very emotional and in a state of grief.

My Spirit people didn't disappoint. A beautiful young man came into my mind and said, 'That's my family at the back!'

He went on to explain that he had been stabbed outside a train station. He was there at the wrong time and was killed due to mistaken identity. He described that he died at the bus stop outside and told me his name and those of his family, who proceeded to moan and groan with each fact he delivered. He was so smart. He even stated that he had gone with the family back to Jamaica a couple of months prior. He said that he was present when his ashes were blessed by the village priest. They were all crying and laughing and displaying such heightened emotions. Their clever little boy had brought them so much closure and had alleviated, I hope, some of their pain.

I was chuffed. At the end of the service the grandma came up to me. I was sure she was going to give me her deepest thanks, as most did but she said in a strong West Indian accent, 'You may be bringing me my grandson but I saw the devil in your glass. The water had the blue sprites of hell swishing around and you gulped them all up. Come with me sister.'

She then grabbed me and took me to where her family were. They proceeded to chant an apparent *Devil go away* song. They then tickled me all over with turkey feathers and said that my soul had been saved. Wow. I laughed all the way home. They put a bit of a dampener on my link with their boy, but as long as they were happy, all good!

I recall doing an Evening of Mediumship at a church in Leytonstone. I came to this lady and knew I was with her right away. 'Are you Margaret?'

She jumped and said, 'Yes!'

I then searched in my mind to see who had told me her name. I saw a light manifest next to her. As I stared into the light, I saw the name Bill,

'Bill is here for you, my love.'

She didn't respond how I wanted her to. She kind of half smiled but there was a spark of worry in her eyes.

'He is saying hello to you.'

'No, you are not with me.'

'Oh, is there anyone else here called Margaret who would know the spirit man Bill?'

Silence.

'I think I am with you darling; he says that he loved your cooking and especially your apple pies.'

'No, you are not with me.'

The man next to her, obviously her husband, then said, 'Isn't that Bill our neighbour, love?'

She looked at her husband with irritation and said, 'No, no it's not!'

At this point I put her in the *scaredy cat* category. It happened regularly where the recipient suddenly loses courage and fears spirit contact, bless them. But Bill wasn't backing down,

I then said, 'He is talking about his dog. He was a black Labrador and the dog is with him now.'

'No, you are not with me.'

'But he had a black Labrador, love!' exclaimed the husband.

This went on and on. You may have learned by now I am like a dog with a bone so I kept pressing her. The husband was clearly understanding everything but she did not want to play ball with me.

Even Bill, bless him, was standing next to me bellowing in my ear: 'It is her! That's Margaret!'

In the end I had to cut the link. I was very disappointed and so was Bill!

During half time I went to the quiet room. After five minutes there was a knock at the door. I opened the door to see Margaret standing there.

'I have to be quick as I have told my husband I have gone to the loo.'

'Ok,' I said, feeling a little confused and a little agitated with her not having taken my message.

'It's about Bill,' she stated with a heavy sigh. 'I am not going to lie, I was panicking Nicky. I am so sorry I kept saying no when the message was clearly for me. You see the problem was, I was petrified Bill was going to say something in front of my husband! When he said he loved my cooking, I thought *oh blimey the game's up*! You see, I had an affair with Bill for years.'

We fell silent for a while but then I couldn't hold it any longer, I smiled and so did she and then for some reason we both burst into laughter. We just couldn't stop.

'God Nicky, I thought you were going to ruin my marriage! We went through a phase where we couldn't stand each other, so I leant on Bill more and more. I still love him now but his death led to my husband being the same man I had first married. Oh, what a muddle!'

'Your secret is safe with me!' I winked. To be fair I did use this story as an icebreaker at my dems to make people feel at ease. My line was: 'So, if you say no to me, it means you are having an affair!'

I was doing an Evening of Mediumship on a barge of all places, in Leigh-on-Sea, Essex. I have never felt so embarrassed in all my life with one of the messages. It takes a lot for me to go red, but this was so funny. A Spirit man had come to talk with his wife in the audience. He was very witty and really cheeky. I'd bet he hadn't changed one little bit since going up to Heaven, but then again, they rarely do.

'He keeps saying the name Charlie to me.'

'No, I can't take that name,' she replied looking puzzled.

'He definitely is saying that name, darling, and saying how nice he was.'

'Nope, not at all.'

This Spirit man would not move on until I got it right, so this exchange went on for about five minutes. Then in my mind, he manifested himself in full and held up his hands and made a squeezing motion with his fingers. He then wrote up on a board NICE CHARLIES.

When the realisation hit me, I declared out loud: 'Oh my God, he is saying *nice Charlies*, I think he means my boobs!'

The whole crowd doubled up with laughter and I went crimson. It was a golden nugget because his wife said if an attractive girl walked past, he would say, '*Nice Charlies!* with a squeezing motion to make his wife laugh. I was being chatted up by someone in the Spirit World!

I have also delivered the line, 'Can I feel your boobs,' to a lady when I was supposed to say, 'I can feel a problem in your breasts!' It was only a cyst which brought so much relief to her.

In Bethnal Green a lady's mum came through, Beryl. Now Beryl was a tough Eastender and there were no holds barred with her language. Remember I said I had to watch my airs and graces; well, this took me to my limit!

Beryl said: 'Tell her that her husband is the biggest wanker I have ever met!'

Oh no, this couldn't be happening.

'Your mum says she didn't get on too well with your husband?'

You are never supposed to change what the spirit person is saying but sometimes you have to adopt a little tact!

Daughter: 'Well, not really. He can be a bit difficult.'

Beryl: 'A bit difficult? He is a tight fisted, fat ugly pig of a man who needs a pole up his arse to get moving!'

Oh, please!

Me: 'She is saying sometimes he needs a bit of encouragement to get up and about.'

Daughter: 'Yes, sometimes.'

Beryl: 'Sometimes? He is a lazy twat who doesn't even work. He just sits watching the telly, drinking beer and taking all of her money, the good for nothing....' The expletives then flowed magnificently.

The daughter looked at me as I stayed silent, waiting for Beryl to stop swearing and ranting. She had a look of puzzlement on her face as I was taking even more time to think of how I could relay it all nicely.

'She is saying that she doesn't agree and that perhaps he should help out a bit more?'

Daughter: 'I suppose.'

This then led to another rant by Beryl. I was getting more drained by the minute, trying to keep this message as polite as possible. Thank the Angels the recipient's brother was sitting near her.

'Oh, for God's sake Vicky. Your husband is an arsehole, stop defending him, mum is so right and I bet she is saying it a lot more colourfully!'

This led to laughter throughout the hall.

Beryl: 'Get rid!'

I thought I can't do this anymore. 'Your mum is saying, *'Get rid!'*

I didn't know it but it was a golden nugget moment.

Daughter: 'OMG, get rid was the last thing she said to me before she died.'

Me: 'Who is Dave?'

I saw the name written up in my mind's eye.

Daughter: 'That's him, my husband.'

Beryl relaxed. 'She's got the message, love. Good on ya!'

Me: 'Well I don't think I need to say anything more.'

Brother: 'No, you don't!'

Again, the audience laughed out loud. I think much of it was from nervousness but I felt a lot of them knew this man and had known Beryl. Suffice to say about eight months later I got an email from the daughter thanking me for bringing her mum through. It gave her the incentive to *get rid* of her husband and she was now happier than ever.

In Hornchurch, Essex, I was preparing myself for a message that I thought would no doubt be welcomed. I could see the lady in question and knew her husband was with me.

'Darling, I am coming to you. I have your husband here.' I could see she was older and might be fragile, so I was going to go easy on this one.

'Oh, okay.'

Oh, she is clearly grieving him, I thought, *she is so quiet and obviously overwhelmed.*

Underwhelmed actually, I found out after delicately saying: 'Are you okay if I work with you and your husband?' I had on my most empathetic expression.

'No, tell him to fuck off and go back to wherever he came! He was a git. I want to talk to my mum instead!'

Again, the whole place rocked with laughter. I asked this poor man to go away. Later on in the dem, her mum came and gave a beautiful message that included claiming she was making her husband's life hell up there! Which brings on a salient point that if you do have someone come through who you do not want to talk to, good Mediums can move them on so that you don't get upset. We either get another spirit family member or cut the link because, nine times out of ten, a family member who you do want to talk to will make contact during the dem.

So, as you can see a lot of laughter was had in the centres and churches. Laughter is key to raising the vibration of human energies, meaning we can blend better with the spirit frequency. That is why I have chosen to take a light approach in this book. It is not out of disrespect, it is as our spirit loved ones would want it; hopeful, light-hearted and a celebration of their life. The last thing they want are dark clouds, devastation and bleakness.

However, we cannot ignore the miracles and absolute proof that Spirit people bring via Mediums. In the next chapter you will see the pure brilliance of spirit communication and unquestionable evidence that we survive.

Full. Stop.

CHAPTER 8

The Miracles that Spirits Bring

———— ★ ★ ★ ————

My confidence continued to surge as I visited each centre and church. My personal readings were also soaring to a different level. I was a channel for the Spirit World every single day and the more I relaxed into this new way of being, the stronger and more gobsmacking the messages became. I decided to take a recorder just for my own personal spiritual growth to a dem at the Epping Spiritualist Church. I have never shared this link before, but now is the right time. It illustrates how amazing the Spirit World can be and how beautifully they can communicate through a Medium. What follows is a reading word-for-word, that I gave a lady in the audience, using N for me and R for the recipient.

N – I have a lady here who connects with the name Mary. She has a lady standing next to her who is called Beth. Mary has chestnut brown hair, beautiful brown sparkling eyes, a well made-up face where she used a powder compact, which she tells me someone still has. She says that she is a mum and wishes to talk about Phil. (I could see her so clearly in my mind's eye it was ridiculous, every pore of her skin, every eyelash surrounding her wonderful eyes).

N - Can anyone connect with this lady?

R - Lady puts her hand up

N – Hello darling, you understand all of this?

R - Yes

N - She is now telling me the name Karen

R - That's my name

N – Oh, that's good! She is telling me that she passed with cancer and I get 49/50 for some reason.

R - She did pass with cancer, she was 49. She died just before her 50th birthday.

N - Oh bless her heart! She gives me the 27th of the month.

R - That's the day that she passed!

N - I go to the stomach for the cancer and she tells me the funeral was at 2.35 pm.

R - Oh my God, yes that's correct!

N – Wow, okay. Can you understand Beth next to her?

R – Yes, that's my mum. Mary is my son's mum-in-law.

N – Oh, she has just said don't call me Mary, call me Maz!

R – Yes that's right, everyone called her Maz.

N – She tells me that her favourite colour was green. She likes my shell necklace and I see shells and stones around her neck.

R – Yes, that was her favourite necklace

N – This lady speaks very softly. Unlike me! She was a very patient lady and tolerant of people, sometimes too much so!

R – Yes that's right.

N – She now takes me to the month of July and mentions Phil again.

R – That's our grandson. That's when he was born.

N – She tells me that this was her first one, but she didn't miss it! He was 6lb 7oz.

R – Oh my God, yes that's right!

I am gobsmacked by now!

N – Really? Is that right?

R – Yes, yes it is.

Everyone started to mumble in the crowd now, having heard one amazing bit of evidence after another. Karen just kept gasping and looking at her friend next to her. I was on such a high, it was ridiculous!

N – She tells me she is here to help your son and her daughter as well. Who is Stacey?

R – That's my daughter-in-law, Phil's mum.

N – Darling, was she poorly? I feel down this region? (Stomach/groin)

R – Yes, she had cervical cancer.

N – Yes, I feel this but didn't want to voice that, rather you say it. Maz tells me that she has been with her every step of the way and is very proud of her for getting well and will be there always. Also, I feel the name Julie.

R – That's my sister.

N – Darling, I could be with this lady all day. She is like me, likes a bit of a natter! I would like, she says, for you to pass on to everyone that I am here and happy although I am frustrated that I was taken a little too soon!

R – Thank you, thank you so much - that was literally amazing!

N – Darling, it's my pleasure. I have tried to see what mum wanted to say but she let Maz talk and has gone!

R – That's okay.

N – Also, I have a black dog here. Quite slim, beautiful face and great big floppy ears. I can't hear his name but can see the first two letters: TY.

R – His name was Tyson. He was very well loved.

N – Well, all I can say is he has just turned up with a lot of love as well as the other two lovely ladies.

R – Thank you, bless you.

N – You are welcome, my love. I will leave all of their love with you.

This was a landmark reading for me. It showed me how I was advancing in my ever-developing energy. I felt so happy getting such accurate messages.

If you relax into a reading with no ego, you really can get whatever information you want. I had learned that I could go back and ask questions and get the right answers. I went back in my mind to search for Beth, asking where she was, but was told she had gone. I also knew that you could never order who came through, you just had to accept the communication of whoever was there. Maz had used this opportunity to let her daughter Stacey know that she was aware of her baby. She also wanted Stacey to know that she had seen when Stacey had got cervical cancer and that she was with her, bringing her strength and support. Maz was totally aware of everything that had happened and through her communication, proved it. The names, dates, birth and weight of the baby just blew me away. This reading set a precedence for my teaching. It wasn't too long afterwards that I started doing circles for people and training them in my own right. When I taught, (you will know this if you were a student) I adhered to the following mnemonic:

P – Passing condition

R – Reason for coming to communicate

I – Identity/personality/memories/job/hobbies/interests

S – Sex of the spirit person

M – Message: what did they want to tell their recipient? Why are they here?

I used to make every student who had a link with a spirit cover all of PRISM before I asked them to end the communication. I can see no reason why any Medium cannot do this, as well as find answers to certain questions. I felt like I was in my old job as a police officer. The spirit person was a witness, I was the officer asking the questions and the audience my jury! I would not settle until I got every bit of evidence I could from the spirit person to prove their existence. I cannot abide these Mediums that say: 'I have a father-figure here, or a lady who wants to say...' How vague is that?

I would like to also add that the 'jury' can be your support or your demise. If their energy is rubbish you won't get any readings close to the one I have just shared with you. Also, the *'no'* people. They are just the worst kind because when they say no before you even finish your sentence, it chops the energy in two, breaks your confidence and that is when the tiny demons of doubt start to ebb away in your mind. It causes the link to become diluted or blocked.

I learned that the word '*no*' was irrelevant a couple of days later, in a centre in Gravesend. It made me vow never to let a person block the reading by saying no again! It reminded me of the London club I went to with the smoking, stout-drinking monsters.

The crowd there had never seen me before so, as tends to be the case, I could feel the up and down looks and the scepticism being sent towards me. The first couple of links were very slow and the audience members were responding to my connections with: 'no, don't know, could be, possibly' - it was that sort of energy. I was embarrassed and could feel my neck and face on fire with the humiliation. The person who ran the centre had hailed me as the best Medium in the country. I certainly felt I wasn't living up to that billing. Then it happened, this most magnificent energy entered the room. I could feel her standing right next to me. In my third eye I saw this darling child looking up at me. She then pushed visions through my mind that made me feel sick. I could see her in a house fire. She was showing me the scene, I could smell the smoke and the materials burning.

'I have a little girl here, possibly about 5 years old. I absolutely know that she passed in a house fire. It is so unusual I am going to put it straight out there, does anyone understand this?'

Absolutely nothing. The spirit, previously smiling at me, was crestfallen. All you could hear was an expectant silence in the crowd accompanied by a solitary cough. *Fuck*! This was getting so hard. The girl was pleading for me to carry on pushing her presence forward but, to be honest, I let my ego get in the way. I ended my link with her out of embarrassment and told her no one understood who she was. The first part of the evening concluded and I went straight into the toilet to get some space following the dreadful readings. My sanctuary, the toilet! I always ended up in a cubicle begging the Spirit World to help me out and this was no exception.

'Please!' I was hissing. 'For God's sake help me out; granddad, dad, anyone - come and bloody well save the day or I won't be invited back here!'

In the doorway of the toilet cubicle, I knew the little girl was standing there. She had the angriest expression on her face and I knew that I couldn't ignore her.

'Right Nicky' I said to myself. 'Get your big pants on and sort this out. No more taking no for an answer! You have been right all evening, go kick some arse. Come on little 'un, let's get you acknowledged.'

So, I literally marched onto that stage and said: 'Ladies and gentlemen, I'm sorry but I have to insist about this little girl. She needs to be heard. She died in a house fire. She is about five years old. It wasn't her house she was in when she passed. Her brother, sister and mum got out but she didn't. Please help me and her out here. Does anyone understand this?'

It was one of those days where I just couldn't find my recipient, so it was up to them.

I then saw this sheepish hand go up. Yep, just as with the London one, I wanted to shake her!

N – Do you understand this

R – Yes

Why didn't she say yes in the first half then?

N – The little girl?

R- Yes, she's five and died in a house fire last night. Her mum is my friend.

At last!

N – Do you understand the name Emily?

R – Yes that's her sister's name.

N – And who is Lynn?

R – That's my friend's name, her mum.

N – And Keith?

R- Fucking hell, that's her dad's name!

This delivered some laughter, which lifted the energy to the rooftops. The little girl proceeded to tell me everything, she was so happy! She described her mummy and daddy, where the house fire was and special little memories that the lady had to pass on to her friend. It was so emotional; everyone was crying in the room by the time I finished, including me.

The little spirit girl was elated and instructed me to say, 'Tell mummy and daddy not to cry. I am okay and in Heaven. I just fell asleep, it didn't hurt.'

That ended me! I was trying to hold back the tears as I said this last piece to her mum's friend. In fact, as I write this now, I am going to dedicate the next chapter to how bloody amazing children and babies are at coming through to a Medium. After this amazing contact every message came flying out and what remained that night was spot on. I was invited to come back time and time again to that wonderful place. I also learned that if my bosses, the Spirit World, insisted that they wanted to bring a message through, I would never back down again. At the end of the evening, the lady who answered to the little girl came up to me. She said, 'I am so sorry Nicky but a Medium once told me that it takes at least 6 months for a spirit person to come through. That's why I thought it couldn't be Jade.' What bloody nonsense! Spirit people come through when they know you are ready to hear from them!

'Darling, please don't worry. I will tell you something now. I went to do an intimate evening at a place in London at a person's house. Straight away a lady called Anne came through. She was the girl's step mum. It was 8 PM and she said them: 'Don't think you are getting rid of me that easily!' She had died at 4PM that day. So, whoever told you that my love, are talking pants!'

She laughed. 'Oh, okay. I will pass the message on when I think it is right to my friend. Aren't the Spirit people amazing>'

I paused. 'Yes, they are, they never cease in amazing me.'

The Spirit World doesn't do time in a human sense. They do energy and know when it is the right time to communicate, visit and make their presence known. Never forget that. Jade obviously needed to get through right then and there, bless her beautiful heart. Children, our darling babies that are taken too soon. Just because they are young when they pass it doesn't mean their souls are. For this reason, they are the most amazing communicators going.

With each demonstration providing its own learning point, it was like I was in my own spiritual bootcamp, being trained by something unseen but magical. The following week was another gobsmacking lesson: I received my first foreign spirit person.

By this time, I had had a building built at the bottom of my garden, which I called *The Enigma Sanctuary*. At my centre, I was doing circles, workshops, group and private readings. It was booked out for the year. My work just never stopped. That lot up there just wanted me to go everywhere and promote the afterlife. I have to admit, my work did take over my life and this was the time that I should have paid attention to balancing work and play. I continued on the ride unabated and bathed in the glow of my name and reputation. Everyone wanted to say they had been trained by me and they would swarm around anyone that knew me. I was being put on an invisible pedestal and quite frankly I loved it. It helped keep my demons of not particularly loving myself at bay.

I will always remember watching *The Sixth Sense with Colin Fry* and *Best of British Mediums* at the London Palladium and thinking, 'I want that!' I wanted to be the best of the best and have the ability to reach millions with my proof that the afterlife was real. They always say, be careful what you wish for.

One day in the Sanctuary, a beautiful girl had come for a private reading. She was nervous when she sat down but we were soon in the swing of things. Her granddad came through. I kept seeing Istanbul in my head and asked her why. She stated that is where her granddad came from, he was Turkish. This would be interesting, I thought. He had already stated names of the family, his memories with his granddaughter, his job and other amazing facts about the family.

N - What's the word *derya*?

R – Oh my God that means sea, he adored the sea.

N – Right, and now he is telling me *Yenikapi*...

R – That's where my dad lives! It's by the sea in Istanbul.

N – He is saying, sorry if I say it wrong, *sevda* or *sedgi?* Is that a name?

R – No, it means love!

N – He then says *Kis torun*, or something like that.

R – Jesus, that means granddaughter!

This is what finally broke her; she realised that she really was talking to her granddad.

For me it was another breakthrough. From then on, any foreign Spirit people connected in English but would pop a few foreign words in just to prove it was them. I loved it! I even had my guide Julianus channel through me speaking medieval Italian mixed with Polish! So don't worry, they all come through using a language that the Medium will know.

With more learning under my belt, I must show you some examples of how amazing Spirit children really are and how they helped me to grow even more.

Read. On!

CHAPTER 9

From The Mouths of Babes

———— ★ ★ ★ ————

Before I start showing you some of the glorious examples of spirit child communication, I firstly want to mention another upgrade I received. I was getting very frustrated with having to describe people in my mind's eye. So, one day before I was doing a reading, I said, 'It wouldn't hurt for you to actually show yourselves, rather than making me work harder to concentrate on your energy!' Well, ask and you shall receive.

The next lady who came in for a reading had only been sat for about five minutes when, amazingly, her dad came through. And I mean literally. As I began describing him, he started to push his upper torso through the wall right next to me. I was so excited! I just looked up at him and he was there in a transparent state. I could see all of his features, even down to a tiny mole on his cheek!

From that day on, if there was a high voltage energy in the air, the Spirit people would manifest in full or just their faces. They normally appeared to my right. So, no doubt any of you reading this who have watched me work will always see me look to the right. If they didn't show themselves fully, I would see a bright purple orb which directed me to where they were standing. With this new attribute under my belt, Mediumship got a little easier!

One day a married couple came to my home for a reading. The wife looked apprehensive and the husband was sceptical. It didn't take him long to relax however once his daughter Emma came through. She showed me her running in a sports day at school before everything went black. She was only thirteen years old. She was an excellent communicator, telling me what she had been buried in, her siblings' names, what her bedroom looked like and providing a lot of other information that was understood by both parents. I was so moved by her as she had passed with an awful condition that is quite common, SADS, Sudden Adult Death Syndrome. It's a little bit like cot death but in those who are grown. Emma had been so full of life and then, *puff,* gone. I decided to do a charity night at my local Indian restaurant. I wanted to make money for SADS as it was not government funded, which I found astonishing. This was to be my first public show not in a church or centre. I was beyond nervous and so invited one of my friends for moral support, an excellent Medium by the name of Ronnie Buckingham. He did half the show with me and the place was absolutely packed to the rafters. The raffle alone ended up raising a huge amount for the charity.

Working with a more general audience was a new challenge. For many it was their first time with a Medium, requiring more patience and focus on my part. I had to continually repeat what I was saying for it to sink in. There were a lot more sceptics and a lot more fearful people that thought you were going to give them a fortune teller's reading, so when a spirit person rocked up, they would shit themselves! Having sat there stunned, many warmed up once I started to mention personal things likes dates and addresses and they realised I really was talking to their dead relatives. Overall, I found that you also had to work harder to keep the audience engaged. There is something of a showbiz element to public theatre and hall demonstrations. It requires a certain personality and humour that keeps them laughing, intrigued and entertained in addition to delivering messages from Spirit.

Luckily, I was a born entertainer and so I found a new joy in watching people gasp as I gave them information from the dead. It was a buzz I soon became addicted to. I decided after that evening that I would venture out on my own and start doing public shows in my own right. I was struggling to pay my mortgage with the church fees and knew I had to step up and get myself out there in the big wide world.

I continue to choose charities that I support each year as a way of giving something back. I ended up demonstrating in theatres in Spain, Germany, Europe, as well as all over the UK. I also started doing telephone readings for people across the globe. I worked with many well-known Mediums, resulting in me touring with the late Colin Fry. But let us not get ahead of ourselves and continue to focus on our precious babies.

On top of doing the large major shows, I had been told by my guide, Julianus, to reach out to smaller groups. Intimate evenings were then born, where I would visit people's houses and do a private Evening of Mediumship. I adored these evenings. Most people laid on nibbles and wine for their guests and I brought their spirit family members to them.

There was one booking that I felt a little apprehensive about, where a very large group had booked a room in a community Hall. I turned up to the venue in Kent and could feel a certain tension in the air. The first couple of links were okay. I was aware that I kept looking at a certain woman but so far nothing had come through for her.

I then said, 'I have a nan here who wants to talk to her granddaughter, Kate.' Straight away the lady I had been looking at put her hand up.

'I'm Kate, it could be me.'

'Yep, that's her, I'm her nan,' said the old lady.

The nan gave a lot of information, proving it was her but I felt that I was missing something. Kate didn't seem overly impressed. When people act like this it is because they are new to it, deeply grieving or desperately need to hear from someone else. Or simply it's because they are just plain rude!

'I know what you are thinking, you know she wants someone else,' said the nan to me. 'Tell her I am just getting her.'

N – Your nan says it wasn't her that you needed to come through. She just wanted to relax you and ease you in. She is saying that she is just going to get her.

The whole crowd gasped and Kate's neighbours frantically grasped her hands in support.

I then saw a beautiful young child. In my training I had learned that if a baby was lost in pregnancy or very soon after birth, they would show their image at around three years old so they could be better described. They could also say what date they passed and, if they were two and over, they normally showed me the age they had been at the time. Indeed, this little girl presented as a three-year-old but I knew she had been nine months when she passed.

N – This is your darling baby girl, Kate. She is so happy up there with your nan but knows that you are not happy and that you just want to join her. She says to stop feeling the guilt - it was an accident.

Kate's reply was an animalistic wail, followed by sobbing.

N – Who is Dean?

R – That is her daddy, my husband.

N – Is she Molly?

This then led to her sobbing even louder. Her mum nodded next to her, confirming that was the little girl's name.

I then saw Molly being strapped in her baby seat by Kate in the back of a red car. Kate had got into the driving seat of the car. I felt and saw a huge impact from a vehicle behind and then it went blank. I knew that Kate hadn't fixed the car seat strap properly. My God, how had she lived with that?

N – Mummy you have to stop wanting to come up here. I am very safe and you did not do this on purpose.

How wise was this child?

N – Please be happy with daddy and the rest of the family. You will see me again when you come up, which isn't for a very long time.

Kate couldn't answer; the pain, guilt, relief and shock of what had been told to her made her unravel right in front of me.

We took a break and I went into a private room with Kate and her mum. It turned out that Kate had experienced severe depression since the accident and kept attempting suicide. The accident had happened six years prior. She was living in a permanent state of revulsion with herself. The guilt was all-consuming. I continued to connect Molly to her mum and gave as much information as possible.

Many months later I got a thank you email. Kate was getting better, with no more thoughts of suicide and an acceptance that it was nothing but an accident. She had been comforted in the knowledge that there was an afterlife and her baby was thriving with her great nan. Understandably, she would never get over this tragedy completely, but Molly's message was certainly helping.

Another time, I was doing a theatre show in Norfolk. It was a very large venue, and the place was a sell-out. Just before the end of the first half, a young girl fully manifested on to the stage in front of me. I could see her outline as she showed off her pink tracksuit, which she proudly stated to have been buried in. When no one could take her initially, she started to stamp on the stage with frustration, to the extent where I could feel the vibrations!

N - I'm going to say this information again…

Right kid, give me everything you have. Play it out in my head, I thought and my God did she!

N – Okay, she is showing me the name Donna. I think that is who's in the audience. She went to check on her pony, Snowdrop, and she ran up to her too quickly, causing the pony to kick out and hit her head. It goes dark, so I know she passed then and there. Her name is Ella. Oh, God no… She has just shown me the view from her pony; her mum is crying at the gate as she saw it happen. She had fancy horses with feathers take her to the church at her funeral and wants mum to add more butterflies to the garden with water trickling.

R – Yes, yes, it's me. I am Donna, that's my best friend's daughter!

This woman was practically jumping up and down with excitement.

N - The most important thing to say to mum and dad is I AM NOT LOST!

R – Oh My God, that makes so much sense.

I then went on to bring so much laughter from Ella. She was a joy to work with and said so many things that were spot on.

During the half time break Donna called Ella's mum. She then came over to me and explained why she didn't put her hand up to begin with. Another famous Medium had told Ella's mum that her daughter was lost after she had died and couldn't find her way back home. I was raging. She then went on to say that her mum then wanted to kill herself as then she may be able to go and find her baby girl. I got in contact with the parents and tried to help as much as I could, leaving them in no uncertain terms that their dear Ella was not lost at all.

Amazingly Ella came through again on a different night in a Norfolk venue when I didn't even know her family members were there. After this second reading, Ella's mum created the most amazing memorial garden full of butterflies and a wonderful water feature for Ella. This is a great way to honour your child. It is also a good spot for you to chat with them and reminisce rather than at a grave. No Spirit people hang out at their graves, it's far too morbid! Ella's mum also knew that her baby was safe and well and she no longer felt the need to take herself over. It's yet another beautiful story where the child heals her family and to be honest I have so many it's been hard to pick the ones for this book! As for the Medium, I just wanted to punch her for saying such a stupid thing to such a vulnerable family. Apparently, the Medium was flailing around saying that all the child could see was black and was lost, she then ended the reading, leaving the parents distraught. Jesus!

Another total star was Andrew who arrived at a show in North Essex. He came through to his dad after being run over by a car. His dad had never been to see a Medium before and the shock on his face as his son reeled out one fact after another was a joy to see. The interesting thing that Andrew said to his dad was that he loved to help other children when they passed over. He was like the guardian angel of the young. Now and then I would see his energy show up at a dem and I knew a baby or young child was about to come through. He was helping them connect with me, how awesome is that?

Talking earlier of guilty mummies, I have learned that babies who have been terminated NEVER want their mums to feel guilt. I have had hundreds of babies who have passed this way come through and not one of them is angry or upset. Without getting too deep, we are part of a soul cluster. We have the ability to plan our next incarnations with the rest of our family and the older our souls get the harder the experiences are on earth. So please remember if you are one of those mums, they have planned this all before they had been incarnated. They go on and stay with your family members just like any other child. They also stay with any siblings that have been lost whilst still in the womb or born sleeping. There is no difference, they are all happy and surrounded by unrequited love. You'll see when you get up there, I promise you. I know this because countless times they come through with other family members, saying the date they passed and how long they were in the womb for. It doesn't matter how young they were when they passed, they have a soul that belongs to your soul family.

I have to mention this amazing story where I had tears streaming down my face during the whole reading. I was at my favourite place, The Light Upon the Hill Spiritualist church in Dartford, Kent.

This beautiful boy Jamie came through and all I could see was him wrapped in heavy bandaging and looking up to a ceiling where sparkling things were dangling as he couldn't move and could only look up. Some disgusting little shit had thrown a firework down his back, I was horrified. Jamie told me that he passed from his burns and he was in hospital for 4 -5 days and that he was nine years old. Incredibly no one could take him, no one put their hand up. I sent my thoughts back to James and asked him for more information. He showed me a scene that literally broke my heart, a nurse was holding him very gently as he passed to the Spirit World. I asked for any nurses in the audience and an older lady raised her hand in shock suddenly remembering the little boy. What was so magical about this lady was she was off duty and felt a need to go in to see Jamie just before she went home. A call had gone into his parents to say that he had gone downhill. The nurse, Betty, knew that he needed human contact and comfort so she gently cuddled him and spoke to him as he passed. He wanted to come through to thank her for being there with him as he went to Spirit. His parents had literally just left to get a shower and see their other children.

It taught me that Spirit people never forget their carers and nurses who were there for them in their final hours. What a beautiful soul Betty was, being there for Jamie just when he needed it. He had found the chance to say thank you that night. It was nothing short of awesome.

Mums and dads should never have to bury their children. It goes against every law of nature but, sadly, it happens. It rips through a family with devastating consequences and many never recover. I just hope in this chapter you can see that your babies and children are safe, well, and are looked after by their spirit family when they go up. They are never alone; they are never scared and will always be watching over you.

To add to my spiritual training, another thing was just about to be brought to me concerning baby passings that knocked me for six.

Simply. Awesome.

CHAPTER 10

The Esoteric Cord

---- ★ ★ ★ ----

Here, I want to take the subject of children and babies one step further. After I had been introduced to child energy, the babies and children started to flood in. This was a new experience for me as I had never been a mum. To be honest, I never wanted to be one and even said when I was only about five years old: 'Mummy, do you know when girls grow up and have babies?'

'Yes,' she had said, frowning a little, no doubt wondering why a child of my age would broach this subject.

'I don't ever and will never have them, so you won't be a nanny with me.'

'Oh okay, perhaps you will change your mind.'

'No mummy, sorry I won't!'

My mum used to remind me of this conversation throughout the years. I knew I wasn't going to have children. I wanted a career and freedom. I am the happiest auntie ever but being a mum just wasn't for me. It could have been reinforced by my abusive adolescence and feelings of abandonment; I really don't know. To say this at five, though, was quite the insight into my future!

As Mediums, our own experiences tend to attract certain spirit genres through. For instance, my brother Richard can bring through spirit children all day long as he is a dad of four. I struggle as I don't have that maternal empathy or experience. I normally get murder victims, traumatised deaths and mums and dads as I recognise their energy from my old job and own personal loss. However, as I was getting upgrades covering all manner of subjects to add to my spiritual utility belt, babies were the next lesson to be learned.

I had just finished doing a dem in Shoebury, Essex, at a lovely spirit centre I attended regularly. A young girl in attendance approached me, I think with her mum. She asked to have a word with me in private. She firstly apologised for what she was going to show me but didn't think I would be too upset as she knew that I had been a police officer. She produced a photo of her darling sister, who had been born sleeping. She was such a tiny little thing but perfectly formed. I didn't register it to begin with but the girl asked what the silver rod was that was coming from her sister's tummy, or for those that know, the solar plexus area.

My initial thought was it might be a fault with the camera or the result of a lens flare. The girl explained that they had taken many shots after this one and could not recreate the silver rod in any way shape or form. It was 3D in appearance and glowed a bright white. It was like a thick rope spiralling up to the ceiling. I had to admit that I didn't know what it was but I said that I would try and find out and get back to them. To my shame I was so busy that I completely forgot to get back to them or even research the subject online or with my guides. However, when my bosses need to teach me something they will not let it go until I have learned the lesson!

Incredibly, about three months later I was doing a dem in South London. I was having a cup of tea afterwards when a lady approached me. She apologised initially for what she was about to show me. The hairs stood up on the back of my neck. It was like déjà vu and I knew instinctively what I was going to be shown. It was a picture of her darling son, who had been born sleeping. Yep, you guessed it, from his tummy area was the same rod of silver light that I had seen in the previous photograph in Shoebury. I could not believe it. I explained to her that I had seen this before and would go up and ask my guides what it was. I promised her that I would be in touch as soon as possible.

The following morning, I set time apart to meditate. Julianus was there to greet me at my guide meeting spot. We sat on a long white settee whilst I asked him what the silver cord was.

'It is the Esoteric Cord, Nichola. It is created at the time of consummation and stays attached to the infant's soul through the pregnancy. As soon as the infant breathes its first breath, the cord starts to dissipate. When the baby has reached a stage where its parents are nurturing and growing that infant, the cord disappears. It is there as a safety mechanism. If the infant passes and comes back home before it has lived, its soul travels back up the cord and resides with its soul cluster in the Reality Layer. Some infants born with ailments also have the cord attached as some of them pass soon after physical birth.'

Basically, after I came back from the meditation, I likened it to a spiritual umbilical cord. I was astounded and so humbled to have witnessed it visually in these photos. My goodness, what an amazing thing to have explained by my guide. I was so excited to get back to these people and explain what was in their babies' photos! The Esoteric Cord is similar to the thin cord that keeps our soul connected to our bodies. This has also been shown to me by Julianus. In sleep state, our souls can leave our bodies and travel astrally. The thin cord, or soul line, is there so that when we come out of theta and alpha brain wave states and start to wake, our soul can arrive safely. The soul or astral line, from what I have seen, is very fine. It certainly isn't the brilliant silver cord that I have now witnessed several times in baby pictures.

I just needed to add this bit of information as I have noticed over the decades the biggest grief women hold are terminations, miscarriages and babies born sleeping. As the baby didn't have a physical life and didn't affect anyone else (apart from maybe their fathers), women feel like they need to shut up about it after a while and hold it in their hearts rather than talk about it. They then fail to properly grieve their special angel babies. I implore you that if you are still grieving to go and see a counsellor. I know you may feel that you don't need to talk about it but, from my experience, most mums do.

I thought that mentioning the cord might bring you some comfort. So many mums have shared with me their fear that as their babies were so young, they would just disappear. They are not lost; they are not alone and they certainly continue to exist with their soul family in Heaven. I have also been asked if they can reincarnate into another baby's body to the same mum in the same lifetime. I have never seen evidence of this from the angels or my spirit guides, or the babies themselves for that matter. Babies have always told me that they are happy with their spirit family, looking over you and their siblings. Reincarnation doesn't take place for three generations when you get up there, so my answer is no, your baby's souls won't come down into the next baby you have.

Having souls in bodies you might recognise would give room for chaos. From what I have been taught, we reincarnate after many generations so our successors don't remember our time on Earth.

To see another soul in another body goes against all the laws of the Universe. I must say that I have seen reports of babies remembering their past lives and being reunited with those family members who were still alive. When I asked Julianus about this he said it was a 'Universal blip or, as humans would say, an admin blip.' he then smiled and said no more.

Perhaps I am not to know all the secrets of how the Universe works!

Hey. Ho!

CHAPTER 11

Murder Most Horrid

———— ★ ★ ★ ————

As I mentioned in the previous chapter, murder victims came to me quite easily – most likely because of my past career. It was therefore no surprise when the following happened...

Within nine months of me going full time, the media started to get interested in me. I was offered features in spiritual magazines and was even approached by a TV producer. She asked if she could send me a photograph of a child to see what I could pick up. I had no idea that it was in fact an audition for an amazing murder case. The photo was sent via email. It was a very old black and white image of a young boy with glasses. I was given absolutely no information whatsoever, just: *here is a photo, what can you pick up?* I have to say what followed I think was some of the best Mediumship that I have ever done.

As soon as I received the email, I instantly felt sick to the stomach. An immense sense of doom and sadness overwhelmed me. Within seconds I started to get flashes of visions in my mind that were out of control. I quickly grabbed my notebook and started to scribble out what I was seeing. I will never forget what I saw. The young boy was walking along a street on a lovely day that felt like summer. He was then being approached by a van, from which I could hear the voices of a man and a woman. The woman started talking to this boy and, before I knew it, I had a movie playing out in my head of the events that unfolded. The boy was bundled into the back of this van. I then saw a flash of his glasses being left somewhere and a hand picking them up. The vision then switched to a mass of moorland where he was holding the hand of a man.

I knew he was being walked to his death.

A map then started to manifest in my mind, forcing me to close my eyes. I saw a steep path that led down to a gate, attached to which was a sign on a red bit of rope stating: *PRIVATE LAND – NO FISHING.* I saw myself walking along a path and I noticed a lone tree to my left as the land started to form a valley. I knew that I was in a desolate area. I then noticed a stream on my left and a reservoir and dam to my right. Further on there was a dead sheep with a broken back laid over a large rock. I saw as I walked along a cluster of yellow flowers gathered at a stile-type gate. The path then led to a crossing at the meeting point of three streams. About ten feet beyond the little boy's voice said: 'That's where I was left.'

I could then hear the stream flowing and how it bubbled as it met the other two streams. I could smell the peat and the disturbed earth. It had been raining when he was buried. Thank God, he had spared me the actual murder but I knew that he had been strangled. I then heard something so macabre that it chilled me to the core, I heard laughter. The man and the woman from the van were laughing about the atrocity they had committed.

After I came round from this vision, I quickly drew a map of what I had seen. I was trembling as I did it and sent this information off. Within an hour I got a phone call.

I was being invited to go to Saddleworth moors in Yorkshire as a programme was being made on the murder victims of Myra Hindley and Ian Brady. The photo they had sent me was of Keith Bennett, the one victim that had never been found. The Executive Producer of the programme, Simon Moorhead, was currently in Hollywood but would soon be returning to the UK. We were all to go to the Moors and I was going to be tried and tested like nothing I had ever experienced in my life.

The time came and a large crew travelled up to Saddleworth moors in Yorkshire. I had to confess that I had no intimate knowledge of the crimes apart from there being a number of children who were murdered by the monster couple back in the 60's. I did not research a thing as I knew it would impair my natural intuition. I was not told what was going to be expected of me, so on the way up I enjoyed a lot of banter with the team. Amongst them was an historian and a geologist.

As we got onto the moors, my interest piqued and I leaned forward in the car. I can only describe what happened next as being taken over by a force unknown. We were in the middle of the moors and I screamed: 'STOP, NOW!' The car pulled up and I got out into driving rain and wind that nearly blew me off my feet. I started to march from the road onto the moor. I had no idea why I was doing this; I just had an immense need to walk. I then stopped abruptly and all I remember is that I could feel my feet vibrating beneath me. I knew I was standing over a grave.

'This is where Leslie was found,' I said automatically. I had no idea who Leslie was. I then started to walk to my left and as soon as my feet started to vibrate: 'Pauline.' I then turned around, marched back to the road, crossed it and said after walking for a few minutes: 'John.' The only thing the team confirmed was that I had correctly identified each grave site for three of the children that had been murdered by the couple. I couldn't even remember how many the pair had murdered. I was emotionless. I felt like I was a robot programmed to trace and find. I got back into the car and asked the driver to turn around. As we went back on ourselves, I then requested that we stop again in a nearby car park. I got out and straight away began walking down a sloping path towards a copse of fir trees. I could not believe my eyes when I got to the bottom because, right in front of me, there was a metal gate saying *PRIVATE LAND NO FISHING*, hanging down on a red rope. I found myself then walking to the left on a gravel path. My steps quickened as I caught sight of what I now know to be Greenfield reservoir on my right. I was following the map I had seen in my head a couple of months beforehand, after studying Keith's picture. I looked up at the lone tree groaning in the wind. When I heard the trickling of the stream to my left it sent the hairs up on the back of my neck. I was getting closer. I remember the small talk of the team, but I was not really acknowledging them. All that mattered was I knew I was getting closer.

I was gobsmacked when the next vision manifested straight in front of me. There, on a rock, in the middle of the stream was a dead sheep bent backwards. I was almost running now as I knew I wasn't far from where I needed to be. The cluster of yellow flowers nailed it as I crossed over an ancient stile. Up ahead three streams met. I felt delirious, almost hysterical as I got to the point where the waters joined together. I walked along the stream that led to the right, hopped over it and ran frantically to the spot that I knew Keith had shown me. I stopped directly on it and found myself invaded by mixed emotions of fear, sadness, happiness and relief. It came out in gasps and happy sobs. I knew he had been buried here. After using his equipment, the geologist confirmed that a shallow grave had been in this spot but had been washed away by high water levels over the last sixty years.

I don't care what has been said in the media or who has professed to what, I am adamant that is where Keith is, along that watercourse. There is no way on this earth I could have come up with a map that was so unique that led me to this certain spot out of 29 square miles of moorland. The same with the graves, I went straight to them without hesitation. To this day I still don't know why this spot was never acknowledged publicly. Most probably because the documentary unfortunately never hit the screen. I have no idea why it didn't.

The following day, I was taken to another location, an estate somewhere in Manchester. As usual no one said a word to me. I had to volunteer all of the information I picked up psychically and no one would say if I was wrong or right. In fact, they just said, 'Okay'. So, I literally had to trust these children's messages and trust that my psychic visions were on point. The car stopped in a road on an estate lined with unremarkable houses. As soon as I got out of the vehicle I doubled over with painful cramps and swallowed back bile that had risen into my throat. I was freezing cold but sweating profusely. I then heard a young girl crying followed by a young man screaming. I couldn't take what I was hearing. I clapped my hands over my ears and knelt on the pavement. Vomit kept rising to my throat and I repeatedly wretched. After a while I managed to stammer, 'Get me out of here.' I looked up to a gap between the houses and knew that I was at Ian Brady's property, or at least where it used to be. I couldn't cope with the energy. I stated that I knew where they had taken me and did not want to go back. I have to say that I had never been so violently ill near a physical location before.

It took me many months to get over those trips to Saddleworth Moor. The dreams and the overwhelming feelings that clung to me after every visit stayed with me for some time.

I assumed having been a Major Investigation Detective in the police that murder victims were quite comfortable in coming to me. They knew that I could handle it. This was apparent when I was holding a circle in my sanctuary one day. We were doing a Halloween group meditation, it was the 31st October 2006. I thought I would have a nice escape to the Spirit World and enjoy a relaxing time, but as soon as I linked in there was a girl looking at me. She was soaking wet and standing by a small pond by a stream. She looked like the woman from the horror film *The Ring*, with straggly long dark hair. I knew that she had been killed and I knew that her body hadn't been found because she looked lost and not at peace. She showed me the word *Ipswich* and then just proceeded to stare at me, shivering. I then saw the name Nichol, so I assumed that she was called Nicole.

When we came out of the meditation I said to my students, 'There is going to be a body found as I have just seen a murder victim. She showed me Ipswich so I know that she will be found there somewhere. Keep a look out.' I then went on to explain the area and her description. Imagine what a fool I felt when week after week passed and nothing came up on the news. I felt a little embarrassed as I was so sure she had been killed. Continuing to meet up with my students, I chose not to mention it anymore!

Then, unbelievably on the 9 December 2006, when I was staying with my friend Jo in Suffolk, I got a text from one of them. *OMG! Turn the telly on, it's the murder girl!* I ran down the stairs and switched on the TV, and there was her face, the girl I had seen.

Her name was Tania Nicol. She had been found in a brook near Ipswich. I couldn't believe it, when I thought back through the days, I realised she had come to me the day following her murder, having gone missing the night before. Her body hadn't been discovered until six weeks later. It was also amazing that I was already in Suffolk, so I drove straight to the location. It was obviously blocked off by the police but as I gazed down the road, I knew that she had been found on the right-hand side by a bridge where there were some trees next to an industrial unit.

This was the first victim of the Ipswich serial killer Steven Wright, even though she was the second girl to be found. I started to get information from the girls all the time predicting where the other victims would be found and information about the suspect. I sent it to the police, but after hearing nothing back I didn't bother anymore. With much relief I ended up doing readings for some of the victim's family members. At the time I had no idea they were related as I did the readings over the phone with just a first name as a point of contact. One of them was related to Tania Nicol and wow, did she look amazing now she was up in the Spirit World and healed! The other one was Paula who also looked wonderful.

Over the years many victims have come to me, children killed by paedophiles, women killed by their boyfriends, men killed randomly (wrong place, wrong time), along with well documented cases such as the model, Sally Ann Bowman, who was killed in Surrey - one of the victims of Peter Sutcliffe, The Yorkshire Ripper. I had so much information on Sally that I phoned the police incident office. The detective confirmed that there was a lot of correct information that hadn't been released to the press but after that phone call I never heard from them again. I wish we could be like America and have psychics used on major cases, as I know we could help. When I was a Detective a lot of the psychics that called in were just judged as crackpots. If the information was good, it was deemed that they had knowledge of the case rather than having psychic ability! The cases were harrowing when I was in the job, but now I see the other side, the side where the victims are healed, happy and free.

I need to mention this as I am sure it will bring comfort to anyone reading this that has experienced the misfortune of a loved one being murdered. I promise you that they never suffer. They always show me the details unfolding as if they are stepping away from their body and looking down on the scene. I never feel their pain like I do if I am channelling, say, someone who had a heart attack. I have learned that the soul is taken from the physical body just as the trauma is about to take place. So, no matter how horrifically your loved one died, they did not suffer, they just watched the demise of their body from a distance. As soon as their physical body passes, they are whizzed up to the Spirit World for healing and cleansing of their trauma by the Seraphim. The Seraphim are one of the most ancient orders of the angel hierarchy. Part of their job is to cleanse traumatised souls at the Fountain of Life in the Celestial Garden in Heaven. So, think of them by a fountain getting healed rather than the misery of their murder.

A spirit boy showed this beautifully when I was doing a dem in Kent. I cannot tell you how traumatic this link was for me and I have to say the audience sat there just as numb as I was, with silent tears running down their faces, to match my own. He came through looking amazing and said that his name was Alfie. He looked so very young and vibrant. He was shrouded in a beautiful green light, which to me represents Archangel Raphael's energy, the Archangel of Healing.

N – I have a boy here... hang on.

I was smiling as I first blended with him but then he started to show me how he passed from this world. My smile faded as he took me along a canal where I saw his bike left on its side. I knew he was leading me to where he had been killed, I just knew it. He made the killer look like a black shadow as we both watched him being led away by the man. The man was known to him and his family and was a paedophile. Alfie's body was discovered a little later and the whole town was left mortified. Alfie's parents were in the crowd, my God how brave they were to sit there as their amazing son told them not to worry. He said that he had been healed by the beautiful ladies singing (had to be the Seraphim!) and lived with Nan and Granddad up in Heaven. He assured them and the whole audience that he didn't feel a thing when it happened and it was just a distant memory. He was so sad that his mum and dad were still miserable and wanted them to heal just as much as he had. He also said that the man in jail would have to face himself in Heaven. I shit you not, there was not a dry eye in the house, he was only nine when it happened. He was talking like he was 90 years old with such wisdom and grace. What an angel.

For the record, murderers get the worst Karma ever when they go up. I have seen what happens to their souls and believe me, it is beyond grim! That will all be fully explained in my next book, *What Happens When We Die*! There are so many murders that I could mention here but it would be the longest chapter ever! So, I will leave it there.

The next chapter is a little cheerier. I share with you the most amazing stories where the Spirit World actually saves people's lives!

Simply. Amazing!

CHAPTER 12

We Also Save Lives

———— ★ ★ ★ ————

I must whizz you back to Chapter Three, when Catherine first presented me with my gift of prophecy, along with being able to see auras and ailments. When I view ailments in people I either feel it in my body where their problem is or I just *know* where their issues are or what illness they have. I see a vision like an Xray and where I see the colour red, that is where the problem is. I focus on an associated area and can then see what type of problem it is, a lump, a cyst or even cancer. My brother, Richard has honed this ability to perfection. He has far stronger intuition when it comes to health and identifying medical problems.

I have learned over the years that if the illness is terminal, I know that I cannot help, just comfort. I remember a while ago emailing a lady who was dying. She had found me on my YouTube channel and wanted to know what to expect when she passed. It was a total honour for me and very humbling as I described what would happen in her transition to Heaven. The day she never replied, I cried and prayed for her.

This reminds me of a very poignant reading I did for someone in my sanctuary.

A beautiful lady walked into the door, very well dressed and looking exceptionally healthy. When I first greet a sitter (as we refer to them), I really am not looking at the person, I am already sending messages up to the Spirit World asking to bring people down for a connection. She was a lovely young lady and within minutes of her arriving her first friend Steve came through. He had passed with cancer and was so happy! He said that he was relieved it was all over and was having endless parties up there with his friends and family. After about twenty-five minutes, four friends had come through to this lady, all of whom had passed with cancer. There is always a particular reason or person people come for when having a reading but I just couldn't nail what she was there for.

'Is it all okay so far?' I asked

'Yes, absolutely,' she replied calmly.

I continued to bring in so many people who had passed with cancer. They were joking about their bald heads and the laughs they had whilst having chemo. It was such a strange reading. It then hit me. I looked at this lady with my third eye and I got it. She had terminal cancer. All these people were friends and those she had met when she was having her chemo treatment.

'You wanted proof that there is an afterlife didn't you, darling?'

Her eyes shone with emotion. 'Yes I did and you have given it to me. You have described and named everyone that I have lost to this disease, but now I know I will be joining them soon. Thank you, that is the only reason I came to you.'

I can't tell you how deeply the reading touched me, God Bless her brave, beautiful heart.

However, if you are meant to be healed or saved by your spirit loved one or a psychic it is because that is part of your path. That is when Spirit people or my intuition warn those that they are seriously ill. I had a reading booked in my sanctuary for a girl named Donna.

I was absolutely delighted when I saw her come through the door as she used to work at Basildon Police station when I was in the force. I hadn't seen her for years, so it was nice to catch up. I was slightly nervous as I was now presenting myself as a Psychic and not a Detective!

The reading was going exceptionally well, but then I could see red highlighted in her lower abdomen.

N - Have you got a gynae problem at all, Donna?

D – Well I have had problems over the years…

N – No, I mean recently, like really bad pains or anything that feels wrong?

D – No, not really.

N - I can see a mass there, hun. I think there will be a bleed of some sort. You must go straight away to the hospital or your doctor's as it will turn out bad. I am sorry to say it, but you really must go, you must promise me!

D – Yes, yes of course, I will make the appointment straight away.

I am so glad Donna did! She contacted me about a week later. She had made the appointment and they had found a tumour. They removed it immediately and gave her a hysterectomy. The tumour was precancerous, so there was no doubt it would have eventually led to being a threat to her life if untreated. I love it when this happens.

Interestingly, I have an unknown spirit lady who steps in from the Spirit World if I am dealing with a client who has a medical condition. She is blonde and very bubbly but, apart from that, I have never seen what she properly looks like and have never asked, it just doesn't seem right. She was a nurse when she was last down here and pops in as soon as something medical comes up. She has even told me what medications people should be on and the correct name of the medical condition, along with the affected parts of the body. I always, however, tell my clients to see a doctor first rather than completely rely on a spirit nurse's diagnosis! My nurse has obviously chosen to do this work whilst up in the Reality Layer.

It makes me laugh when my clients say to their doctors, 'Nicky Alan, a Psychic, told me to come here!'

That's exactly what a man called Mark did, telling all and sundry that I had saved his life! It was his spirit dad really that had done it but it did make me feel so proud! Amazingly, just before I started writing this chapter, Anita - Mark's wife – sent me an email after 11 years of no contact, thanking me for giving her 11 more years with her darling husband that she never would have had if it wasn't for my message. So, I thought, you know what? Let Mark tell it in his own words…

The years leading up to my illness were punctuated by highly stressful situations in my life.

My brother had been gravely ill, my mum was in the advanced stages of dementia and I had separated from my wife in the lead up to an unpleasant (if there is any other kind) divorce.

Although I thought I was dealing with these problems reasonably well, it wasn't until Anita came into my life and eased my burden that I began to realise what a toll it was all taking on my health.

As she helped me to deal with things (particularly with mum), and my brother regaining his health, the drive to carry on fighting against all these challenges slowly began to unravel. Perversely, as so often happens, once extreme stress was removed from my life, I began to go downhill.

At first, I noticed that I was feeling tired all the time, which is bad enough for anyone, but as a builder carrying out physical tasks, it was becoming increasingly difficult to stay awake throughout the day. I also had constant slight discomfort in my side which I put down to a strain.

It was around this time that I asked Anita to marry me. She had come into my life and shown me unconditional love, and it slowly dawned on me that she was the person I had been looking for all along. A soulmate who cared for me, listened to my troubles and helped me rebuild my life. I fell deeply in love with her. We decided on a date in November 2010 to get married.

In the summer of 2010, Anita saw that Nicky Alan was holding an Evening of Mediumship at our local village hall and was keen for us both to attend. Anita was (is) highly interested in spiritual matters. While I did believe in the presence of some sort of spiritual existence, it would be fair to say that I was slightly more sceptical, but I was curious so along we went.

Unbeknown to me, Anita had taken along a selection of photos of my late parents and her late grandparents in her handbag, along with my dad's wedding ring which she told me to put on as the event started. As the evening progressed Nicky turned her attention in our direction and described a gentleman fitting the description of Anita's grandfather and mentioned many things she could identify with. Nicky then said she had a lady (Anita's Nan) and although she was in the background had brought another man with her; Nicky described my dad who she said was standing next to her perfectly, even down to his personality. Nicky asked about a ring, a wedding band, I was amazed as I was wearing it. She mentioned a forthcoming party/event and said they would all be there with us.

Nicky described a scene with books all around the room in piles (I read a lot and had a shelf on the wall with books piled to the ceiling). She then said she was feeling pain in her abdomen, and that this was something that should be checked out, she said she was seeing a 'C' and as I have a nephew who had been recently diagnosed with colitis, I automatically assumed that it was him she was referring to. I had decided that after my recent improvements in my health, I was OK.

Nicky was insistent that it was me that my dad was referring to, and said that my dad was saying, 'Get it sorted Boy.' Nicky said the words in just the manner and tone that my dad would have said it. She asked me to promise that I would seek medical advice, which I did, while not really intending to (as blokes do) still remaining convinced that it must be my nephew she was talking about.

I carried on working - putting my tiredness down to the dissatisfaction with my job, the aftermath of the last few years and ignoring the fact that I should really have spoken to the doctor. As our Wedding Day arrived, I found myself feeling even more exhausted. At one point I even left the evening reception to have a rest in our room as I didn't think I would make it through the rest of the day.

We had a wonderful honeymoon in Cyprus and returned home to a severe winter but I seemed to feel a bit better so I carried on working for the next few weeks, putting my perceived health improvement down to the stress and excitement of the wedding and its preparations.

As the weeks went by however my health began to deteriorate again, it was during this time that the shelf of books in our bedroom fell off the wall making the most horrendous noise. I remember Nicky mentioning the books in her reading. Anita had been constantly reminding me of my father's words and my promise to Nicky. I finally gave in and went to see the doctor. Subsequent blood tests showed that my red blood cell count was akin to that of an eighty-year-old man.

On the follow-up visit, he enquired about the pain in my abdomen, and after an examination referred me to a local clinic for a colonoscopy which revealed a nasty-looking lesion in my intestine. When I asked whether the growth was cancer, the reply was 'possibly'.

I received a phone call from the hospital the next day to let me know that a sample had been taken for analysis, and a few days later a consultation confirmed that the lesion was malignant.

I underwent surgery and the tumour was removed and found to be the size of a small melon. I was told that had it not been removed that day I wouldn't have survived much longer as it was so aggressive. Thankfully it appeared not to have spread; I underwent chemotherapy for six months as a precautionary measure.

Today, eleven years later I am still here and have just celebrated my 58th birthday with my family and my six-month-old

Granddaughter. I am extremely grateful to the Surgeons and medical staff for having been given this extra time - long may it continue.

It has to be said however, that had it not been for that evening at the village hall things may have turned out very differently and I may have let things progress further until it was too late had it not been the echo of Nicky's words that evening.

All that remains for me to do is to thank Nicky for singling me out that night and passing on messages from my dad. I owe her a huge debt of gratitude and to say to anyone else who finds themselves in a similar position to act on any such message, sceptic or not. It cannot do any harm to take medical advice afterwards as it may just save your life as it did mine.

Mark Sparrow

His story made me cry! Thank you Mark for such a beautiful addition to my book. How truly amazing our spirit family are.

On another occasion I was doing an Evening of Mediumship in a centre in Grays, Essex. A man came through saying that his name was Del and that he desperately wanted to talk to his daughter, Dawn, in the audience. He was not mucking about this man. His evidence was straight to the point and completely accurate. Dawn raised her hand and confirmed it was her dad communicating and that his name was Del. It turned out that Dawn was due to go to the hospital the following day as it was suspected that she had bowel cancer. She was terrified. I tried to see inside her tummy but couldn't see anything apart from a little inflammation.

Del said, 'Trust me love, you have not got bowel cancer, I promise you. In fact, buy a raffle ticket at half time and to prove you haven't got cancer, you will win and you will take home flowers that are from me.'

Dawn started to cry, 'My dad always brought me flowers every time he came round.'

'Well, get yourself a ticket and let us see what happens,' I said excitedly.

Now I was bloody terrified! What if she didn't win anything? What was I going to do then? Well, I couldn't change the message and I had to trust the Spirit World implicitly, so I had to go with it! As each number got read out at the end for the raffle, my heart thumped just that little bit more but, blow me, she won the last prize! It was a chrysanthemum plant and, amazingly, it was her favourite colour. She skipped out of that hall knowing she didn't have cancer. A couple of weeks later she emailed me, she had been diagnosed with IBS!

Another amazing example where, yet again, a spirit person saved a life was when I was doing a dem in a hall in Dagenham, Essex. It was very similar to Mark's set up. A man had come with his wife and he didn't really look that impressed to be there! However, his dad, Harry, came through for him and provided Jack with some lovely memories. He then became serious.

N – Jack, I know you are stubborn but you must stand your ground and demand a scan. Your dad is insisting that there is something wrong in your kidney area.

R – No, I had a scan there recently, it was clear.

N – No! I have to say you must go back. I can see red in that area and your dad is stamping his foot telling you not to be an idiot, you must go back and insist that they check again.

Poor Jack's wife then nudged him with her elbow as if to tell him to promise me he would go back.

I watched him sigh.

R – Okay, I will ask them for another scan.

Unbelievably, the first scan, perhaps because of the angle of other organs and the bowel at the time, revealed nothing. After Jack's wife nagged him, he demanded a second scan and a large tumour was found on his kidney. It was cancerous but, luckily, they removed it and after a bit of chemo he made a full recovery. Again, if it had been left to grow, it most probably would have been terminal.

My last story still leaves me with chills now. I was doing tabletop readings at a centre in Basildon, Essex. They were an excellent training ground, conducting one reading after another. It helped me to change links and deliver messages really quickly in fifteen or twenty minute sessions. A young lady came and sat in front of me, looking totally miserable. I assumed that she was grieving for someone who had passed. Her name was Lisa and as I blended with her energy, I felt an immense sense of emotional pain. Of all the people to come through, it was an old friend of hers that had jumped in front of a train. I had vague links with her family members and couldn't understand why someone came through who really didn't seem that important to her.

N - Do you want me to carry on with your friend, Lisa?

R - Yes, yes please.

N - Not your nan?

R - No, I want to hear from her.

This poor girl had committed suicide and went on to explain that even though she had wanted to die, she couldn't bear to watch the pain that she had left behind. She had suffered with severe mental health and wished perhaps she had tried to get more help rather than jumping and ending her life.

She then said:

N – Think about it, do you really want to do this? Do you want your mum to suffer? How about you go and get that help that you need?

The words had just come out without me thinking about it. They then sunk in.

N – Oh my God darling, you want to kill yourself!

She shuffled uncomfortably.

R – I was going to do it when I got home tonight, to be honest. I have everything ready but now I am going to go to the hospital instead. I thought no one wanted me here but after hearing from Shirley, I must try and fight.

She had said it so matter of fact that it sent a shockwave through me, bringing tears to my eyes. That simple message had stopped Lisa from taking her life that night. Shirley had stepped in and taken over the reading as she knew exactly what Lisa was going to do. Lisa did surrender and ask for help. I was so pleased to find her at future meetings looking happier than I had ever seen her.

So, you see, our loved ones in Heaven do know we worry about our health as well as those we have lost. When they can help or intervene, they certainly will! I have so many stories like these, I could fill a whole book with them alone.

I had my life saved by my granddad on one occasion. Not only has he and other family members saved my life, but they have also comforted me and warned me of things throughout the years. In fact, I feel like they never leave me, my spirit family. I was in St Lucia on holiday. I woke up in the middle of the night with really bad stomach pain. I went into the toilet and started vomiting. I heard a voice behind me, it was my granddad's.

'It's your appendix bursting Nichola, you need to get to the hospital.'

I jumped when I heard the voice. As I was shivering and sweating profusely and in so much pain, I thought that I was imagining it. As if to answer this he said, 'Nichola, you are not imagining me, you need to get to the hospital now!'

I went into the bedroom and woke up my partner at the time and told him that I had to go to the hospital. He said rather abruptly, 'Nicky if it was your appendix, you would be in agony.'

'Yeah, but my granddad said.'

'Well perhaps he got it wrong, you would be doubled over.'

'I am, I'm in agony.'

'It's just food poisoning. Take some paracetamol and get some sleep.'

Grumpy old git!

The following morning the pain hadn't abated. Despite it feeling like it was stabbing me, I tried not to moan as I walked to the restaurant for breakfast.

'Nichola!' I heard my granddad's voice.

That was enough for me to instantly turn around and head straight to the reception and ask for an ambulance. My granddad was right, my appendix was bursting. The doctor stated that if I had left it any longer, I could have died. If it wasn't for my granddad I would have not bothered, I would have just taken pain killers and thought that I had really bad food poisoning. I was laid out on a table and given a spinal tab as I had told them I had problems with normal anaesthetic. They then proceeded to give me an emergency appendectomy whilst I was awake. It was horrific.

After the surgery my head was in agony. The doctor had ruptured my spinal cord and I was losing cerebral spinal fluid through the tear. I have never experienced pain like it. I had to remain upside down on my hospital bed in an effort to try and help my brain bathe in the leaking fluid. As soon as I laid flat the blinding hot pain that hit my skull made me almost pass out. After a week or so the doctors said they were going to try and inject a blood clot into the tear as I wasn't getting any better. There were risks of paralysis and even death. That afternoon I had sent my partner back to the hotel to get a pad of paper. I was going to write my last will and testament.

As I lay there alone, I said, 'Granddad, if I am going to be okay can you give me a sign, please.'

I then fell asleep and dreamt of my dad and my granddad walking me towards a blinding white light and, as the light abated, a huge angel surrounded by green light stood before me.

I woke up and said, 'If that wasn't just a dream let me know. Was that angel real?'

As I said this, I looked out of the large window that I was suspended upside down by. A white feather the size of one belonging to an ostrich feather blew down on the breeze and stuck to the window, right next to my face. It remained there. I couldn't believe it!

When my partner came back, I said that I didn't need the paper and that I was going to be okay because I had received a sign. The following morning, the day of my operation, I woke up feeling very different. The pain wasn't so bad. I buzzed the nurse and she came and levelled the bed out. To my great surprise, I could actually sit up! My head was still very painful but nowhere near like the agony I had endured during the last nine days. A further scan revealed that the hole had healed itself overnight. The doctors were perplexed but I knew I had been healed by an angel. I spent another month or so in St Lucia as I had to remain flat until my cerebral fluid was restored. Nothing like being ill in the Caribbean sun!

From then on, my connection with the angel realms grew as strong as with the Spirit World. They had a louder more commanding presence so I could tell the difference when they were communicating. I now had both realms by my side, but that meant two bosses now! They didn't come into my life full-time though, until a few years later – as you shall see.

I have had more emails and messages that I can mention where Spirit people have saved their family's lives. Spirit granddads have woken their granddaughters in the night, only for them to find the house on fire. Spirit mums pushing their daughters to go to hospital for an ache that turns out to be life threatening. Spirit children waking their parents and telling them that their baby brother was choking. The stories just go on and on. If we are not supposed to go up to the Spirit World on that occasion, our spirit loved ones will intervene and will nag you with signs and communication until you get yourself sorted! Some call it fate, some call it divine intervention, I call it spirit family and angels saving us.

These communications got me thinking. How could the Spirit people know that their loved ones were going to be okay? How did they know what was going to happen? How could we predict the future together? I went up in meditation and this is what I was told.

Life. Plan!

CHAPTER 13

We Can See Your Future

———— ★ ★ ★ ————

My guide Catherine was the first to bring me the upgrade of prophecy. From the last chapter you will have seen that Spirit people can say what is going to happen in the future as well. How is this done? How can they see what hadn't happened already? How can they be so sure when we can change our minds and have free will? These were the questions that I had in my head when I went up to the Crystal Palace in meditation. In my mind I walked past my white sofa and through the patio doors which is my visual meeting place for Spirit and guide contact. Everyone who develops is usually shown a meeting place in their mind where they will connect with Spirit. I continued along a path and straight away Khan, Catherine and Julianus joined me. Catherine and Khan linked arms with me and before I knew it, I was in a new chamber at the Crystal Palace that I had never seen. In front of me was a swirling mass of energy of every colour that you could imagine. I could feel my body hum with its energy. Now, I am not going to get too deep into the workings of the Crystal Palace and its dimensions, as I will be documenting this place in a later book.

'Where are we?' I asked as I watched the twirling colours.

'You are at the hub of the Universe; this is its source,' Julianus remarked. 'Here you can connect into its energy. As we are all joined as one intelligence, we feel when the Universe hurts, we feel when the Universe rises in triumph, we feel its pulse of life.'

He then showed me when I dreamt of being in a street in New Orleans, wading through water and a shark passing me by. This was the day before Hurricane Katrina hit New Orleans. The main street was flooded with sea animals. I then saw 9/11 as the first plane hit, followed by the death of Princess Diana. The light bulb moment came. I was feeling the spikes of energy in the Universe when something hit humankind that caused a huge reaction. So now I understood why I felt the things I did that took place in the Universe. Sensitives feel other people's energy, so when thousands of people react the same way to an incident, we feel it like a huge wave of emotion. The same happens for planetary happenings, a huge surge of energy will hit us if we are honed to that frequency. I just couldn't work out how the Spirit World, Guides or Psychics knew what was coming in our lives. This is what I was told.

In short, we all form part of a soul cluster - a family of souls. We stay within that cluster for eternity. Our soul mate always has a close relationship with us in every incarnation, whether the experience turns out to be good or bad. Before we reincarnate, we all agree a life plan and create landmarks in our human experience that we want to go through. i.e., death, divorce, births, pain, happiness - whatever the case may be. We agree to have these experiences with our soul guides, as we are in Eutopia in Heaven and want to have human experiences on Earth with a bit of grit! The older our soul, the harder experiences we choose to have on Earth. If we sway too much off our life plan, our guides will bring us back by creating a *Tower Moment* (in Tarot, The Tower card is when everything comes crashing down or changes our life in a second). This is so they can get us back on track with our planned human experience. Guides and our soul cluster who pass before us have access to our life plan and know what is going to happen next by seeing our landmarks. If we find ourselves in turmoil or lost as a human, our loved ones will send us a message via a Medium to tell us what the future will bring, helping us to get through our *Tower Moment*. That is how they can tell what is in our future, it is that simple.

To prove a point, within days I had my first prophecy when doing a dem in Rayleigh, Essex. My predictions always come out of the blue through claircognance (Clear Knowing) when I predict something with no spirit communicating. I just say it without even thinking, but I know it is one hundred percent true. If the Spirit person is communicating, they show me the prediction though pictures or words using my Clairvoyance (Clear Seeing). For instance, a baby in their arms means they are due to be born. If the baby is standing next to them holding their hand, it means the baby has passed. I also see a ribbon, pink for a girl, blue for a boy.

I was speaking to this young girl whose family was in the audience. Her nan was chatting away and was so excited to say hello to her daughters and grandchildren. After a lot of fun, she then showed me a baby in her arms, the ribbon was pink.

N – Oh how lovely! She is so excited about the baby! I can see what sex the baby is, do you want to know? She is also saying the baby will be born prematurely in October but don't panic, it will only be about three weeks early and they will be fine!

The girl's face dropped and she just stared at me. Her mum's head swivelled like in *The Exorcist* towards her daughter, sporting a rather shocked expression.

Oh Shit! None of the family knew. I had put my foot right in it. There was instant tension in the air. After what seemed a bloody eon, she quietly replied:

R – I only found out I was pregnant last week; the baby is due in November and…

She went silent for a moment.

R- I haven't told a soul!

There was a huge commotion coming from the family members, given they hadn't a clue she was pregnant. The nan had spoiled the surprise. After a very dodgy few minutes the mum broke the tension by laughing, but the poor girl remained mortified! Following the show, I apologised profusely and now know to keep my mouth shut and talk to expecting mums in private!

In October she emailed me to confirm that the baby was indeed born three weeks prematurely. It had indeed been a girl, something I had shared with her in private after the show but she hadn't wanted anyone else to know.

Another amazing one was when a girl, Gemma came to see me for a reading. I quickly ascertained that she was desperate for a child. However, I saw red areas around her cervical area and knew there was a problem that she needed treating. I established that she had complex gynaecological problems and already had an ovary removed. The doctors had stated that she would be unable to have a baby.

N – Well I am sorry but I disagree with your doctors, I just know that you are going to have a baby next Christmas and you will call her a Christmassy name.

Gemma didn't take too well to what I had told her.

R – You are giving me false hope and I don't appreciate that. They have told me there is no way I can conceive with all of my problems.

I took a breath, went deep into my intuition and felt I was right, despite what Gemma was saying.

N – I disagree.

I then saw her nan appear by her side. She gave a lot of information that identified her. She said that her name was Rose.

N – My intuition is saying there is a baby coming and you have already said you are not planning to adopt, so let us ask your nan.

I closed my eyes and I could see her nan with a Christmas hat on holding a baby surrounded in pink ribbon.

N – Right darling, I am not wanting to give you false hope and my God I hope that I am right but even your nan has told me you will get pregnant, so stop stressing and by Christmas you will be holding your baby girl in your arms.

Gemma still looked sceptical as she gave a weak, 'okay.'

I was a little stressed after this reading, I have to say. What if I was wrong and ruined this poor girl's life by giving her false hope? I hated being put into this position by the Spirit people!

The following Christmas… I really don't have to tell you, do I? I had a photo emailed to me from gemma holding her baby, Holly!

Talking of Christmas, this has just brought another beautiful story to mind. I was at Hornchurch and I had just linked with a lovely girl called Kelly, who wanted to talk to her mum. It turned out that her mum had waited 14 years to get a message from her daughter! Kelly was an excellent communicator and got straight to the point. Her mum, Irene was so worried about Kelly's dad - he needed serious surgery that would save his life.

She was terrified that she was going to lose her husband on top of losing her daughter.

N – Mum, don't worry, the surgery is going to be done by Christmas and Dad will be with you for a long time after that.

R – No. that can't be right as that's only two months away, we haven't even got the right doctor for him yet.

N – Mum, LISTEN to what I am saying, it will be done by Christmas.

Kelly was adamant and kept driving this home but her mum wouldn't have it.

N – Darling. this is for the future. just let me know when it happens!

I said this as we were getting close to a family argument! Kelly would not back down. She then showed me some bows on a dress. This was really clever because she was showing me pictures as a short cut. It turned out that they lived in Bow, London! She continued showing me many pictures that, when I stopped and focused on them, allowed me to work out what she wanted to say. She loved communicating with me in this way, it was like playing *Catchphrase*, the TV show!

Incredibly, Kelly's mum emailed me in August the following year. Her husband had undergone surgery that saved his life and the name of the new surgeon that did it? Dr Christmas!

My name at this point was reaching radio stations, TV producers, Magazine editors and journalists. My profile was rising to higher levels and it seemed everyone wanted to talk to and talk about Nicky Alan. The firm 'No's went to the TV psychic channels. I did not want to sit for hours on end where customers were being charged exorbitant fees on a premium line. They never gave up asking, I never gave up saying yes.

One of the most dramatic predictions was when I was being filmed for a new TV programme called *Street Seer*. The auditions for the show were being held up in London near St Catherine's dock. I had to go against many established and well-known Mediums. It was a new spiritual TV channel that was being set up and I was going to go around the streets of Britain doing readings for strangers. I was so proud of myself as I got the job after a day of different tests and scenarios. We only did one day on location of filming though as there was a disagreement with the executives over money so that went nowhere after all my hard work.

For the life of me, I cannot remember the town we were in when filming! I was asked to approach people in a high street and ask them if they wanted a reading. I went up to this lady in a wheelchair. If I remember rightly, I think I brought her nan through. Her nan gave some cracking evidence but there was a particular bit that made me nervous.

N – You are going to walk again, you know.

R – What do you mean?

N – You are going to be out of that wheelchair and you are going to be walking around. A new medicine is going to come on the market and a new doctor is going to put you on a trial, and by this time next year you won't be needing the wheelchair.

I have got to be honest; I was panicking. What a massive thing to say to someone who couldn't walk! I didn't want to give her false hope but I had to trust her nan, I just had to. She started to cry and couldn't thank me enough. I prayed that I had got the information right. In this day and age, many Mediums do not make any predictions during a reading. They make it clear on their social media platforms that they will not predict medical conditions, pregnancies or anything that can get them into trouble. I think this is because we have followed America in suing people if we are not happy. It seems some Mediums are uncomfortable doing predictions in case they get taken to court! However, it is a bit of a slap in the face to Spirit if you don't trust the information and that's a shame.

Winding forward to the following year, I was doing a dem in Ongar, Essex. I was starting my introduction when a lady stood up and said, 'Excuse me, sorry, I need to interrupt you!'

I thought that she was going to hurl abuse at me. Everyone turned to look at this lady and the crowd fell silent. Which way was it going to go?

'I need to tell you all that Nicky gave me a reading last year.'

Oh crap, what is she going to say?

'I was in a wheelchair and she told me that I was going to get a new medicine that would get me back to standing and walking again. I am standing here now to prove to you that she was totally right and that the Spirit World is real! Thank you, Nicky, I cannot believe that I walked into this show tonight, you are a God send.'

The whole crowd erupted into applause and I started to cry like a child! I was so happy to see her standing there. I did not recognise her to begin with, but my God how magnificent is the Spirit World with their predictions? She looked so happy to be standing there and proud to have told the whole crowd about her journey.

I recall that I was doing a telephone reading for a lady who was desperate to move but the house had not been sold despite being on the market for ages. She asked me if she was going to move soon, where it would be and what the new property would be like. I thought, do you know what, in for a penny! I told her I was going to go silent. I asked the question in my head; *show me the house she is moving to.* Straight away I saw a house and, after providing some details, asked her to confirm that wasn't her current home that I was describing. She said it wasn't. Great, I thought, as I took myself around the house and the area. It was in a beautiful leafy suburb, there was a lovely pub further down the road and I could feel that the place was named after a tree, although I couldn't work out which one. In the end, and after a lot of mind focus, I saw the word SYCAMORE and knew that this was either the name of the new home or the road it was in. I described the windows, the colour of the door and told her that it would be the eleventh hour and then, BAM, the move would take place really quickly.

It amazes me how much faith some sitters have in Mediums because when the house, or shall I say when *SYCAMORE* house came up online, she immediately told the estate agent that she would put an offer in, subject to viewing! Indeed, it was last minute and when she moved, she told me about the pub at the end of the road and all of the other details I had predicted.

I am not stating that I am some fortune telling guru, but I do believe Spirit people give the information or I sense the information if it really is a lifeline for the recipient. Sometimes I can't predict a thing!

So yes, just a few examples of how Psychics and Spirit people can predict your future. It is truly amazing stuff, isn't it?

My prediction upgrade had been completed by my celestial bosses. The next lesson was all about what happens to people who take their own life.

Going. Early.

CHAPTER 14

We Wanted to Go Home

———— ★ ★ ★ ————

There is always so much stigma around suicide and when someone decides to take themselves over. It was particularly hard in the early days to cope with these spirit people coming through and murder victims as they were traumatic to describe and I didn't have my police colleagues to debrief with after the fact. As I was getting more sensitive with each passing day, it was a challenge to stay neutral and not just collapse in a crying heap when delivering words from a suicide victim. I learned to stay separate from what I was saying but sometimes, especially with children I cried with the sitter and didn't care.

After a traumatic link I would take myself off alone after that session and do a quick healing visualisation where I would imagine Archangel Raphael showering me in pure green light. Only until I was completely bathed in the light would I then open my eyes. Curiously despite me not liking green, especially because my dad died in a green van, I started to paint walls in my house green. My bedroom now is sage green and I adore the colour. I feel subconsciously that the colour heals me whilst I sleep. I also write out all of my emotions and the trauma in my soul journal, hence why I have such detailed clarity when I share my experiences with you. It also proves a fantastic vessel in me purging myself of any trapped trauma or emotions surrounding a particularly hard reading.

In my first days of doing 'Intimate Evenings' which were Evenings of Mediumship in people's homes, I ended up going to a very fancy house in London where the group were all of the Jewish faith. I was somewhat surprised they were having me there, to be honest, but they all made a joke of having a secret evening! I remember bringing this lovely boy through, who I knew had taken himself over. Spirit people who have done this always sit in the background, fearing I may judge them or that they are going to cause even more upset by communicating with their family. I always encourage them, as they have just as much right to come through as any other spirit person. You could cut the air with a knife as I brought him through. I wasn't aware at the time that committing suicide is a sin for Orthodox Jews and brings shame upon the family. This further calls into question why they invited me in the first place and I assume they thought I was just a fortune teller and wouldn't be so accomplished at spirit contact. To begin with, the mother would not acknowledge her son. It took some time to state that I shouldn't be there at all anyway so to accept the love of a son who had committed a mortal sin wasn't really going to change to the situation. I was there and this boy wanted to talk to his mum!

Eventually she came round to the idea. Josh was a superb communicator and gave his mum so much evidence of his survival in the afterlife. You could see her physically relax as she got more and more information from her son. I am not going to lie; it did infuriate me that initially she wasn't going to acknowledge him. It was like he was some sort of devil. The hurt in his eyes was so evident as I saw him in my mind desperate to talk to his mum. I do think religion has a lot to answer for! In the end everyone was elated and this beautiful boy got to explain everything to his mum and I feel both of them got some peace that night.

Very early on when I started to bring people through who had taken themselves over, I started to see my ex partner Ryan's brother, Duncan. He was a very positive, lovable man but he hadn't coped well after his partner had left him. It wasn't the first time she had cheated, but this time he'd literally had enough. He was found hanging in his garage. I found out the hard way on the night he did it. My house at the time had a bathroom downstairs. It was such a pain during the night when you needed to go to the toilet. I was going back up the stairs when I looked up to the top hall landing. I was terrified and shocked to see just a pair of legs swinging. I stood on that step for ages as I did not want to go anywhere near what I was looking at. Throughout my whole life of seeing spirit people, I never saw anything horrible or scary so I had no idea why I was seeing this. I got cold and ended up running though the legs and jumping into bed like a gazelle. I pulled the quilt over my head and refused to look out. In the morning Ryan's screams woke me. It was then that I learned that his brother had taken himself over. He had come to visit me in his darkest hour but had not known how to portray something a bit more presentable in his manifestation.

Two hours later that day, my Medium friend Doug called and said, 'You have just had someone go over from suicide, I am so sorry.' I was numb, shocked and still in denial, how Duncan had got through to someone that quick I will never know. Doug described Duncan with incredible detail even down to what he was wearing the night before. He said that he was ok and being healed over the other side. Later, Ryan's dad confirmed what Duncan had been wearing. It was the same as Doug had described.

Duncan, for some reason, took it upon himself to start showing up and smiling when I was working with a suicide victim. It was so cool! As soon as I saw his darling face I would say to the audience, 'Hold on, there is definitely someone coming through who has taken themselves over.' I would then gently encourage the person to come forward and bring their messages through with love and gentleness just like any other passing. For the record, suicide souls do not go to purgatory, they are not punished for taking their life too soon. They go to exactly the same place that we all go to, they just might need a bit more healing than most souls do who experience a natural death. People who commit suicide have mustered the courage to come forward, they do so with great relief in their energy. Blending with them made me understand that most were in torment down here, encased in a body and mind that slowly killed them. As soon as they became separated from that body and human mind, they felt as free as a bird.

The biggest thing that I also experienced was the anger and guilt of people down here, which is a normal part of the grieving process. When it comes to suicide though, these feelings are way more intense. People left behind always say that they should have sensed how bad their loved one was, how desperate they were and that they could have saved them. They beat themselves up for not preventing the death and keeping their loved one alive. The fact is, and this is from experience of hearing the Spirit people who have done this, they were never going to be saved, even if they were found that time. They would have tried it again. These are the Spirit people that had major mental health issues whilst on the earth plain. We have to bear in mind that those that do a reckless act, as a cry for help with no intention of going over, are the ones that can be saved. So, for anyone reading this who has experienced loss through suicide, please don't blame yourself for not being able to save them. The hardcore souls really would have kept going until they got up to the

Spirit World. You would have done nothing but delay the inevitable. Most of them have agreed in their soul contract to go up early, it was part of their destiny. It is almost like a lesson that they wanted to learn in this incarnation.

I was doing a private reading when an amazing spirit lady came to me with no coaxing at all, blowing away all of my preconceived ideas about initial reluctance. Before I even saw her, I could hear the song by Queen, *Don't Stop Me Now*.

'Omg yes I know who that is straight away,' said the sitter, as soon as I relayed what I was experiencing.

This darling spirit woman had taken herself over, leaving the song on very loud on a loop so the neighbours would call the police. She did this so that none of her family members would find her first. After a lot of emotion from both sides, she showed how happy she now was free from the constraints of severe mental health and physical addiction. I thought they would be sad and full of regrets but, no, some are meant to go up at the exact time that they do.

I might add at this point, that suicide is not the answer. If you go against your soul contract, the blueprint that you agreed before even incarnating, you will have to do the same life all over again. This isn't a great option as it holds the rest of your soul family back, rather than having a new, exciting experience.

One of the most emotional links that I ever had with a suicide lady was when I was doing a charity Evening of Mediumship in Corringham, Essex. Duncan had come forward in the way he often did letting me know I had a suicide.

'I'm Sharon.'

The lady was drunk, confused and desperate as she said her name.

'Hey Sharon, it's okay, I know how you passed,' I thought in my head. 'Just give me what you can to prove its you, hun.'

She came through full of energy making me buzz from head to toe. She described herself exceptionally well, including mentioning her name to a group in the audience who were her friends and family. Everything was going amazingly, but I found the more that I connected with Sharon, the more sadness and desperation emitted from her energy. I started to feel rather down and depressed as I was taken by Sharon back to her days when she was lost and traumatised. I watched her rocking in my mind's eye and wail. I could feel the knots of pain in my heart and the nausea in my stomach. My head hurt and spun as she blended with me. The sitters knew exactly why, but I didn't. I am very much an investigative Medium, so when I need to get an answer, I am relentless. I will not stop the message until I know the full picture. I kept asking Sharon why she was so sad in her life. I could sense an air of expectancy from her loved ones as well.

I stood on the stage and said, 'Sharon, I'm not going anywhere until you tell me why you did this and what caused you so much sadness.'

The room went quiet for about five minutes and then, the answer came in the most magnificent way. She showed herself on the stage beaming, holding the hand of her young daughter. You could even hear the stage boards creak as she manifested her energy right in front of me. Lots of the audience's eyes widened as they heard the wood groaning!

The picture became clear, 'I wanted to find my Lily as I didn't want her to be alone.'

Sharon's daughter had died and she desperately needed to go make sure she had made it to Heaven. There wasn't a dry eye in the house, including mine! Bless her beautiful heart. One of the most poignant things she said to her family was, 'I made a mistake, Lily was in Heaven and safe all that time. I now know that I shouldn't have done what I did and I am so sorry.'

Jesus, I kid you not, I had to take a few minutes to get myself together. What a brave thing to do as a mum!

However, a message to parents who have the mortifying experience of losing a child. Please don't go and do the same thing. Your children are safe, they are looked after by your spirit family. If anything, you will break their hearts knowing you have ended your life just for them, when they are safe and well and never lost. I know that the pain of losing a child is beyond anything anyone should endure. As I stood trying to hold it together, I saw a shimmering mist appear to my right on the stage. The mist started to form into a little girl, it was Lily. She started to skip around me as I heard her say, 'Silly mummy!' I relayed what I was seeing and hearing to the audience who laughed with all their hearts. It certainly brought a healing vibe to the room rather than tragedy.

There is the danger, thankfully rare, of people fearing judgement by God or their family in Heaven when they take themselves over. These are the ones that can stay grounded on the earth plane for as long as they keep themselves in torment. By refusing to go up they end up perpetuating their own purgatory.

I had one of these situations and it was a real eye-opener. I was asked to go to a house in Hornchurch, Essex as there were a lot of worrying things taking place in the children's bedroom. I particularly loved doing house clearings as I always saw them as a challenge. Was there going to be a negative energy there or just nan? Unfortunately, 99 per cent of them turned out to be family members wanting to be noticed, I know that sounds awful. I was intrigued with grounded and negative energies and the very rare ones I came across I found myself going back into police mode and enjoying the challenge of moving them on.

Sorry, now back to the house in Hornchurch. Weird sounds, freezing cold spots, bad smells and general paranormal occurrences that were really upsetting the occupants was taking place, it sounded like a goodie.

As always when visiting a home that has problems, I ask for a cup of tea so I can gauge the owner of the home and the energy of the house. Whilst the owners are distracted making the tea, I can zone in on their energy just to make sure they are not creating the problem themselves! I then scan the house, in this case terraced and on an estate built in the 1970s. Not the typically haunted mansion with squeaking doors and cobweb-ridden dank hallways! I could feel no history causing the problem either, where some houses are built on troubled land.

After having tea, I went up to the kid's bedroom. I could feel the energy right away, there was a portal or a door right above the bunk bed. Someone had opened this door and was popping in and out frequently. It didn't feel right, I couldn't get the peace and tranquillity of a visitor from Heaven. I suspected this person had not gone up to the Spirit World and had not received their life review and healing. I sensed that it was definitely a male energy. They felt grounded and still haunted by their own memories of human emotions, pain, guilt, regret, frustration and anger. I also could feel that even though he was not a bad soul at all, his human emotions were being projected into the ether and making the bedroom very uninviting.

I withdrew and looked at the top of the stairs, realising that the man wanted to communicate as he had shown me them as being relevant. I knew in that minute as I gazed at the landing that he had hung himself even though he had done it elsewhere. He then said his full name, which coincidentally was exactly the same as the monster my mum had married after my dad passed.

I shouted down to the woman who owned the house, 'Hun, do you know the name Stuart Perkins?'

She said, 'Oh my God, that's my brother. He killed himself a little while ago.'

It turned out that Stuart had hung himself at the top of his stairs. He felt so guilty that he couldn't look out for his nieces and nephews anymore that he went directly to their house and essentially set up a vigil. As he hadn't received his own peace and healing, he was creating an awful environment filled with all of his demons and emotions. I managed to start a dialogue with him and, by the end of the conversation, he was mortified. He was not aware that his own emotions and the traumatised state of his soul were permeating the room and upstairs. He honestly thought that he was looking after his sister's kids but, having not healed himself, he was making their home a sad and terrible place to live in.

I directed him to go up to the Spirit World and find his family with the help of Julianus who always turned up for clearings. When ready, he could then visit his family down here in this house. It was a very emotional experience as he really was such a beautiful man, who had no longer been able to cope with this life. He honestly thought he was making amends by standing by the children. At least his sister Lin got to have a chat with him before he went up to the light.

Since that day the house completely changed and the kids did not have any other problems. How wonderful was that? Poor Stuart, he had the best intentions but it had been at the cost of his own soul getting the healing it deserved.

Please know that your loved ones who take themselves over do go to Heaven and you will see them with the rest of your family when it is your time.

In the next chapter you will see that our spirit family will stop at nothing to reach us.

Pure. Determination.

CHAPTER 15

We Will Seek You Out

———— ★ ★ ★ ————

There is one thing I have noticed about Spirit people: they will find who they want to get a message to, come what may. It is very common in a reading for a random spirit person to interrupt the proceedings because they know that the sitter knows their daughter! I call these 'Medium messages' where the recipient becomes the Medium themself and passes the message along to their friend or other family member. It does make for amazing proof of the afterlife because you are giving information to someone who hasn't got a clue if it's right or not. They then go and pass the information on and it proves completely correct. I whoop with joy when I get an email days later from the person that the message was intended for.

A great example of this was when a man came through when I was doing a dem in Brixham, Devon. He had passed in awful trauma and was desperate to speak to his partner. She wasn't in the room but he must have been scanning for someone who knew her. Initially no one could take Jason but he was not going anywhere!

I kept thinking to him, 'Find the right person then, love, as I haven't got a clue.'

He was a very cheeky young man but also had a short temper. When I couldn't find the person he wanted I could feel him getting more and more agitated.

Then, bang, he just said in the middle of nowhere 'Kate.'

'Is there anyone called Kate in the room?'

'Yes.' One solitary hand went up.

Thank God, I thought.

'Are you sure that you don't know anyone that passed liked this and is called Jason?'

'Oh my God, Jason! That's my friend's partner!

Yes! At last, the penny had dropped. I could feel the relief as Jason stated fact after fact. I was so pleased that he had found his recipient. Kate sent the message onto Jason's partner and after a few days she emailed me. How incredible is that?

Spirit people see Mediums as huge, towering beacons of light, so when they see a Medium near to someone they know, they want to reach out and make contact. If they are blocked or the Medium doesn't sense them, or there is any other reason they can't be heard, they will not give up. They are unrelenting!

My spirit dad found the light of an amazing Medium called Julie in Dagenham, Essex. He haunted her for days until she managed to track me down through her friend who was a neighbour to my ex-sister-in-law! How incredible is that!

Another time, I recall being in an Italian restaurant having dinner with Ryan. It was one of our local favourites in Southend. Just as we had finished our starter, he said, 'Oh no, you've got that look!'

That look was me staring off to the distance because someone was trying to communicate. I glanced to my right and standing by the dining table was the cutest little boy I had ever seen. He had dark curly hair, was about four years old, and had the most endearing dimple on his left cheek. His smile was intoxicating.

'Hello, my little darling,' I said in my head.

'That's my mummy and daddy there.' He stated quite simply, pointing over to a couple directly across the way from me.

'Oh, is it?'

'Nick, you are not doing this now, this is our time, who is it?' Ryan asked impatiently.

'He is only a little 'un!' I argued.

'You've had half a glass of wine, they are out enjoying themselves, do you honestly think this is the right place to bring up that their dead son wants to speak to them?'

He was right. What was I to do?

'Listen darling, I know that you want to talk to your mummy and daddy but I can't do it now.' He looked crestfallen.

'Find a way to get your mum and dad to me. You can do it clever boy.'

He then disappeared. I couldn't stop looking at the couple but I knew the time wasn't right.

A couple of months later I was serving a church in Southend, Essex. Everything was going along wonderfully when I started to see a little boy manifest in the aisle between the two sides of the audience. I immediately recognised him. As soon as I described him a woman immediately raised her hand. It was the couple from the restaurant. I couldn't believe it. Their clever little boy had found a way to talk to them. After the service I was dying to know how they had got there. They said that a flier had come through the door advertising a special evening with me and they thought they would come out of curiosity as they lived close by. They had never been to a spiritualist church before and felt drawn to come! I explained the restaurant story and they were overwhelmed. How special is that? That perfect little boy had somehow influenced them to come on that night as he knew I would be there.

I remember it was a lovely summer's day and I was giving a reading to a lady in my sanctuary. Halfway through the reading this boy pushed up against my glass door, cupped his hand over his eyes and stared in.

'Rude little bugger!' I thought. It must be the next sitter and she had brought her boy.

'Sorry about that!' I laughed as I looked over to the door.

The lady looked puzzled. I continued my work but the boy was really pissing me off!

'Sorry, I will just tell him to move away from the window,' I said apologetically.

'Who?' asked the lady.

I looked around and the boy had gone. I couldn't believe it, there was nobody there. I went to the door and opened it and discovered there was no one to be seen.

'Oh blimey, it was a spirit! I take it you don't know a blonde boy around three that has passed over.'

'No,' she said.

I think I unsettled her a bit. What was a random spirit child doing looking in on my reading? The exact same thing happened on the next reading. The boy cupped his hands and looked in through the window. The sitter couldn't take him either. What the hell? I went for lunch and knew that this cheeky little boy had come into the house with me. I could hear him giggling and would now and then see his face peek around the door. I kept asking him to come in and talk but he wouldn't.

My last reading was at 4pm. This lovely lady bustled in with such a cheery air about her. Straight away the little boy came to the door, but this time walked through it. I saw the name SAM clearly in my head.

'Darling, before you even sit down, do you know a little boy called Sam who passed.'

She took a brief moment and then said in shock, 'That's my grandson. That's who I came for.'

That amazing little boy knew that his nan was coming and had kept showing himself the whole day. We laughed and cried over his persistence and patience!

I also remember once when I was in the bath chilling out before a show in Grays, Essex.

I started to smell the pungent whiff of burning tobacco. I opened my eyes and a spirit man was sitting on the toilet! I couldn't believe it!

'Excuse me, I'm in the bloody bath!'

'Sorry love, but I want to get in first as I know my daughter is going to be there tonight and I don't want to miss out.'

I was speechless. He spoke with a cigarette hanging out of his mouth. He had a pencil behind his left ear and I could now smell wood shavings as well as the cigarette smoke.

'I'm Frank and my daughter is Louise. She will be in a deep pink top. I'm a carpenter and...'

'Hang on a minute! Bloody hell, I need some rest before I get there. Can't you come back?'

It felt surreal having this conversation with this random man in my bathroom. I was even crossing my legs and had placed a flannel over my boobs!

'Well, yeah I will come back but I came here to beat the queue!'

Bloody cheek! He was right though. When completing my introduction at any dem I can see all of the Spirit people forming to my right in a queue. Some are patient whereas some just jump in with desperation. I told him he would be the first link and to bog off from my bathroom! He disappeared but the stench of smoke didn't!

I got to the venue in Corringham, Essex and, straight away, I saw a lovely blonde woman at the back wearing a magenta top.

'There she is, that's my girl' Frank muttered in my ear when I was trying to introduce myself.

'Alright!' If I was saying it out loud, I would have been saying it through gritted teeth! 'Just shut up and wait!' I hate being rude to Spirit people but blimey, give me a chance.

'Okay, Louise, is that you in the pink top?'

She opened her mouth in astonishment. 'Yes, why?'

I said, 'Your blinking dad visited me in my bathroom when I was having a bath, cheeky sod! He wanted to beat the queue!'

Everyone laughed, but my God what an amazing piece of evidence to start the night with! To be fair, there were about 150 people in attendance so the spirit queue was immense!

I had a similar thing happen when I was driving to a venue in Devon. On the way, a lady came through and said, 'Sorry love, but I am Maggie and I really need to speak to my husband!' She was wearing a lovely cotton lace top, brown wavy short hair and must have been in her 60s. Thank Goodness I wasn't driving, so I could speak to her in my mind!

In true form when I got to the venue I started straight away with, 'I had Maggie in the car with me for about an hour! She wants to talk to her husband and she says it's important to state that she is wearing her white lace top.'

A man started to shuffle around and shyly raised his arm. In his hand was a photo of his wife wearing the white lace top.

'That's my wife, Maggie.' You could hear a pin drop. She was another one that wanted to jump the queue!

On one of my days off I was food shopping in Sainsburys. I was waiting to pay for my stuff.

'Excuse me dear.'

Oh God, not again

'Excuse me dear.'

I could hear an elderly lady's voice in my ear.

'Yes,' I sighed. Supermarkets are particularly difficult when you walk past people everywhere. You can feel their energy, you can hear their thoughts and you can sense Spirit people that are walking around with them. I obviously hadn't closed down properly that day, my beacon of light shining for whoever wanted to jump in on it.

'That's my granddaughter at the till. Please send a message to her. She has a place at a veterinary college in September but she won't go as she fears she will miss home too much and doesn't want to go on her own. Please tell her to go or she will stay on that till for another five years!'

What am I supposed to do with that information? I got more and more stressed as I got closer to the girl.

'Her name is Vicky, dear. Please convince her.'

No pressure there then. It was my turn.

'Hi, would you like any bags today?' I looked down; her name badge read *Vicky*.

'No, I'm okay hun.'

What am I going to say?

'Do you enjoy working here?' I asked, trying desperately to sound casual.

'It's okay.' She smiled.

'I only ask as my brother used to work here.' Lie.

'Oh really?' she asked as she bleeped my things through.

'Hurry dear!'

Ok! I said in my head to her dead grandmother. I felt like the Medium Oda Mae Brown in *GHOST* when she was at the bank and the character, Sam, was talking to her!

'Yes, do you know that he is a vet now! He almost didn't go to Uni though as he was too scared to leave home! Can you believe that? He now has his own practice up in Derbyshire.' Lie!

'Oh, wow. That is so weird.' She stopped bleeping the shopping items through.

'Is it?' I asked, trying to hide the rush of red crawling up my neck with the stress of the lie!

'Yes, I am going to veterinary school in September. I am a bit nervous though about being away from my mates and that.'

'Oh God no, don't be nervous! My bro had a whale of a time and felt so stupid that he was nervous! He has a lovely house now, is on really good money, and has specialised in big animals.' *Ok stop it there Nick, Jesus!*

'Really? Oh, wow, that's just amazing. Well, perhaps I should stop worrying then.'

'Yes, you should. Fear never got anyone anywhere. Go for it and good luck!'

'Thank you, that's really kind.'

'That's it dear,' the grandmother piped in. 'She is going to go now.'

That was it. Boom! The grandmother disappeared and I left Vicky smiling!

Another time when I intervened it got me in big trouble. It taught me to choose my times wisely and not after a load of vodka and tonics! I was in a nightclub with my friends in Southend, Essex. I was a bit tipsy as I hadn't been out for a long time and really needed to let my hair down. I was watching a man on the dance floor who started to push another guy. I suppose as an ex-copper you sense the threat straight away and notice when something looks amiss before most people.

'That's my boy there. Go and stop him. He is gutted, it was my funeral today.'

Oh shit. I'm pissed, not working and now you want to tell me to go to your boy when it looks like he's going to start a fight? I'm sure I could even detect slurring in my thoughts to this spirit man!

'Well, he won't fight anyone if you walk him away and tell him I'm here!'

'He will just think I am some sort of nutter!'

'No, he won't! My name is Ray. I died of a heart attack. I had heart disease for ages and I never got a transplant. The funeral was today and all you have to say is *New York, New York.*'

Why me for God's sake!

So, I put my drink down, heaved a huge sigh and started to walk towards these two men that were now shouting at each other. I went straight to the boy who Ray indicated was his son and said, 'Look, I know you have just come from your dad's funeral.'

He was confused, along with being exceptionally drunk. 'How the fuck do you know, who are you?'

Best be honest here, Nick. Please let the information be right!

'I know you are going to think I am a nutter but I am a Medium. Your dad is here, is his name Ray?'

The boy stopped in his tracks, no longer wanting to punch the other guy out.

'Fuck me, yeah, who are you?'

'I told you; I am a Medium. He told me his name and that he had a heart attack and that he wanted me to stop you fighting as you are a good boy and you would regret it, especially on his funeral day. Don't ruin it! You don't need to get yourself in trouble. He also said to mention the song *New York, New York*.'

This young man could not process what I was saying, he just stood there silently. He then burst into tears and put his head on my shoulders and cuddled me! 'We played that today at his funeral!' he said, sobbing. I had no clue what to do so I just stood there and let him get it all out. Before I knew it someone was yanking my shoulder away from the man.

'What the fuck do you think you are doing, you slag?'

Shit, this has got to be the wife!

'I, I was comforting...' *What do I say?*

This woman started to push me whilst shouting at the top of her lungs. She was also very drunk. I could see I was a few seconds away from getting a punch in the face! Thankfully two doormen must have seen the same thing and came over to ask what the problem was.

'She just talked to my dead dad!' said the young man.

Fuck. Me. I just can't describe everyone's expressions as he said this. Weirdly, my urge was to laugh.

'Let's get you all out in the fresh air, shall we?'

Outside I explained to the girl what had happened and amazingly she had heard of me. It basically ended up with a lot of drunken apologies and me being bought a vodka and tonic.

Never again shall I ever intervene when people are drunk!

Lesson. Learned!

CHAPTER 16

When Two Become One

———— ★ ★ ★ ————

The more that I interacted with the Spirit World, the more that I felt at one with it. When I opened up my energy in preparation to work, I felt that familiar tingle running through my body and my scalp. It felt like I was being bathed in fizzy lemonade. That was my sign to say that my lot up there were ready to rock! I found that my senses were becoming more heightened than ever. I will never know how they do it but I can smell (Clairalience), taste (Clairgustance), hear (Clairaudience), know (Claircognance), feel (Clairsentience), and see (Clairvoyance) whatever they want me to. It really helps to get dynamite evidence across to the sitter. But some of the smells are awful! The worst one for me was whisky, I cannot stand the smell of whisky or brandy. I remember the taste of it being brought to my mouth when I was all dolled up, doing an evening in a theatre with Colin Fry in front of about three thousand people. I couldn't stop gagging and was asking the spirit man, who adored whiskey, to get the taste and smell away from me immediately or I would be throwing up all over the stage! It did often help to have these extra senses brought to me, though.

The clarity of my visions was so amazing! I was doing a dem in Southend-on-Sea, Essex. A real gent of a man started blending with me and said that his wife, Dolly, was in the audience. He showed me a red rose and said it was a special day. I don't like them giving flowers unless they can evidence why. I get so sick of Mediums in churches who say, 'Oh, your mum is here and she has a bunch of flowers for you.' Why would they come all that way with flowers for no reason?

So, I asked him in my head, 'Why have you brought her a red rose?'

'I always did on this day.'

That didn't help!

I felt that he sensed I needed more so he literally walked into my energy. I felt taller and leaner (bonus!) and he was taking me to a hallway. I then saw his wife putting her coat on and opening her purse. She was checking for something. I looked closer and there in the purse was a tiny metal Cornish pixie.

'Tell her about that!' he said rather proudly.

I had no clue what the audience witnessed as I just stood there with my eyes closed whilst he took me to this scene.

N - I have a lovely gentleman here and he is mentioning the name Dolly. I feel this may be his wife as he has a red rose for her.

This lady shot her hand up.

R - Yes, it's me!

She shouted out like it was a bingo hall and she had won the full house!

N - Oh great, darling. Who is Dolly?

R - That's my name. Its Doris but he called me Dolly.

N – Okay, and why would he be insistent in giving you a red rose?

R - Because today…

She took a breath as the tears started to flow.

R - ...would have been our golden wedding anniversary. Every anniversary he always got me a red rose.

N – Oh, darling!

I gave her a minute as everyone murmured and 'ahhed' in the audience.

N - Can I ask you something, my love?

R - Yes, of course.

N - Your husband showed me a scene of you standing in your hallway and putting on your coat before you got here. He then showed me that you were looking into your purse. He must have been standing there with you and took me through the memory. You haven't got a Cornish pixie in your purse by any chance?

Well, the crowd roared when, without saying a word, Dolly reached for her purse and raised something up in the air. It was a Cornish pixie! What a smashing way to prove you are there as a spirit, bringing such precise evidence to your wife!

I recall another evening at a social club in Kent. I had connected with this man who wanted to speak to his wife Diane. He gave such beautiful evidence of their long time together and mentioned family members, pet names, addresses and dates. Yet every time I asked him how he had passed, he skirted around it. As you can probably guess from my earlier chapter, this mainly happens when people commit suicide as they feel ashamed or think I might judge them. I just couldn't fit suicide into this man's energy, though. It just wasn't the way he went. He must have heard my thoughts. I did my investigative Mediumship bit and rooted myself to the spot until I got the answers I needed.

I kept asking him how he had passed and then suddenly my eyes started to water. The smell of cheese - strong mature cheese - was overwhelming and almost making me gag. It was so pungent that I felt like I was chewing on it with the stench going up through my nose and down my throat.

N – Darling, could you tell me why I can smell and taste nothing but cheese?

The audience laughed a little.

D – He died because of cheese.

The audience quietened down!

N – Oh, no! I am so sorry! I don't understand though, my love. Did he choke on it?

D – No, he was addicted to it. He would eat up to a kilo a day and couldn't stop. In the end it damaged his heart and he had a fatal heart attack. I was gobsmacked! How clever was he to make me taste and smell cheese! Also, how tragic was that?

It became apparent that, apart from murder victims, the Spirit people elected to stand in my shoes and make me feel absolutely everything. If they were big, I felt big. If they were tall, I felt tall. It was quite unsettling to begin with, but once it started happening every day, I soon got used to it. Not that I ever did for those who couldn't breathe or had their lungs full up with fluid. The first time that this happened, I really did panic and had to keep sending thoughts to the spirit person to back off. He was so deeply blended with me; he didn't realise that I could feel his lungs filling up as he drowned. It was such a tragic link as he had been on holiday with his wife and they were scuba diving. She had run out of air and his supply was low. The problem was they were so deep that they would have died emergency ascending, so he chose to stay with his wife and drown rather than get The Bends and leave her alone. The emotion that ran through me was second-to-none. The feeling of my lungs tightening and failing to work made me gasp for breath. It was at this point when I started to learn how to get them to back off. I would visualise pushing them away in my mind and saying, *If you don't back off, I will stop the connection.* It worked after that. As soon as my physical body encountered any physical stress, I would send the thought out and they would back off immediately. It was worth it, though, as the family finally got closure on what really happened on that fateful day. Luckily their bodies had washed up on the shore, enabling the family to bury them and feel a degree of peace.

Having this upgrade really did help me in identifying conditions that caused the passing as I would feel heart attacks, strokes, haemorrhages, along with where a cancer was centred. So, it really did help me identify what happened to the person before they passed and was excellent proof for the sitter. People always refer to how someone died, they say, 'I lost my mum, she died of cancer.' It most probably is because it is the final thing, the one causing them to no longer be able to ever physically be with their loved one again. That is why I think it is important to confirm with the spirit person how they shuffled off this mortal coil. It confirms to me and the sitter who they are and how they were taken.

One phenomenon that I absolutely love from Spirit people is when they make me smell their favourite aftershave or perfume. It provides such good evidence from them to their loved one. I was doing a telephone reading for a darling lady called Maureen. Her beautiful daughter Susan had died and she was finding it so very difficult to come to terms with her passing, despite it being some years previously. I particularly love doing telephone readings as you cannot see a thing, you literally have to go with all of your *Spidey senses.*

I took a breath and suddenly I could see that I had lovely long blonde hair. It looked like spun gold as I saw myself brushing it. It smelt of coconut. I then watched a hand reach out for a bottle of *Anais Anais* perfume and spray it on my neck and wrists. As I explained this to Maureen, she went silent. I thought we had been cut off. After a while she stated that her daughter had the most magnificent long blonde hair and that she spent hours brushing it. She would always use coconut oil shampoo and that her absolute favourite perfume was Anais Anais. Diane still had Susan's jumper that she sprayed with Anais Anais for comfort.

I couldn't believe it. Her clever daughter had literally sat in my energy and showed me something magnificent. Susan also went on to tell me that her mum needed to smell her perfume without spraying it, that was when she would know that Susan was stood right beside her. The amount of comfort and closure the reading brought to Maureen was incredible.

I started to become very passionate about this spirit blending lark so I decided to join a trance circle at a local centre. I was a little sceptical, to be honest, but I reminded myself of all the past times spirits had blended with me and sat open-minded, waiting to see what happened. First of all, we did a trance dance. I have to say this is one of the most popular things that I have ever taught in all the years since learning it that day. It was one of the most magical things I have ever done. You stand and allow your thoughts to quieten as you listen to some very powerful spiritual music. As your mind starts to wonder down to the Theta brainwaves, that's when the visions and feelings start. I immediately saw Khan, one of my guides, stand in front of me with a wolf panting next to him. It was so clear and so real that I could feel the wolf's breath on my thigh. He then smiled and disappeared. I was swaying to the mesmerising music and all my guides were standing next to me, holding my body as my arms and legs moved. After a while there was a noise in the room which made me jump and come out of my meditation. I was wide awake and could not get back into the zone. This was unusual for me and left me so frustrated!

I quietly sat down and chose to watch the others dancing and swaying. I could not believe what I saw as I sat there. To this day I know I was brought out of that trance for a reason. I could see orbs of white and blue light, the size of golf balls, wandering around the people, with the people's arms tracking their movements. One of the orbs landed in a lady's hands and I saw her cup her fist around the light, with eyes closed, completely unaware. I knew that orb was the first stage of a child spirit. It turned out that the lady had lost a child, who had come to her during the trance dance! I had never seen anything so clearly in all of my life. When everyone came out of the trance dance, most of them swore that they hadn't moved a muscle. It was a really intense and superb way for me to be introduced to trance work.

Later on, I pushed my thought process down thanks to Theta brainwave music. I felt myself get fatter and my spine shorten as though I was shrinking - a lady called Alice had blended into my body. She was wearing a baby blue cardigan and navy skirt. She started to stretch my vocal cords which made me feel a little uncomfortable. I then saw my granddad in front of me and he made a 'shushing motion' by putting his finger to his lips and said to me, 'Relax Nichola, just go with it, don't panic.'

Seeing him there changed everything, so I did just that, I relaxed. Alice then started to use my voice and call to someone in the room.

'Roger! Roger, is that you dear?'

This person from the across the room then said, 'Yes! Is that you, Alice?'

They then started to have a conversation. I felt as though my soul had been taken to another place. It was like going to sleep as I didn't have a clue what was happening, I just felt like I was in another room watching on from a distance. The next thing I knew I was being gently encouraged to come back, upon which I opened my eyes, feeling a little nauseous. I was given a bit of chocolate for energy and some water to ground me. I was told by the crowd that I was a natural trance Medium and that I had channelled the energy of the spirit of Alice. Roger and Alice were grandparents of someone in the room. She watched her nan and grandad having a full-blown conversation in front of her via two Mediums! I have to say it was one of the most incredible things I have ever experienced. It encouraged me to do trance demonstrations with my students. Julianus would come to the fore. He adored it! He could be a little forthright sometimes and intimidating but he came through whilst I wandered off somewhere and answered the most profound questions. He also regularly spoke Italian and Polish. I have no knowledge of these languages at all, except for ciao, bellissima and grazie! That is about it, but Julianus was fluent and would frequently go from English into Polish or Italian. How fantastic is that?

To be able to blend with Spirit people in this intimate way made me feel and connect with spirit visitors so much more effectively. Without having to close my eyes or go into a deep trance, I was able to feel them and everything they wanted to show me. It improved my Mediumship no end. It could be draining, however, so I really did have to start watching how much I worked. I had such a passion to reunite as many Spirit people with their family and friends as I could, but I was to learn in the not to distant future that this was going to take its toll.

However, as the psychic ride continued, I found that trance was just the beginning. More big things were coming...

Clairvoyant. Machine!

CHAPTER 17

Spirit Guide Upgrades

————— ★ ★ ★ —————

When I see or feel something different that has been given to me from up above, I call it an upgrade. If there was something missing in my arsenal to make me a more effective Medium, I merely asked for it or my guides would provide it. If it didn't get delivered then I knew I wasn't quite ready for it yet.

In my life things were moving fast as well. I am sure our guides and spirit loved ones give us the impetuous to make change when we need it. I had sadly said goodbye to my partner Ryan it was time and I knew it. Someone had complained about the Enigma Sanctuary and I had the council round who ordered me to close it down straight away. I had missed in the work application to ask the neighbours if they were ok about parking. I still feel to this day another Medium reported my centre out of jealousy. I had a year of students booked for courses and no venue, so I had to rent a premises in Wickford which caused a great financial loss. My neighbours were also getting shitty with all of my students attending, so I in those times ran, this meant me moving house. I only moved about two miles up the road as I wanted a fresh start. The house was huge for me just living there but at the time I saw it as an investment for the future. I found that I was struggling a bit with my health. I had lots of gynae issues which were resulting in operations. I was working even when in pain and a couple of days after surgery, I couldn't afford to miss a beat and forgot to care for my body and myself for that matter. I did take some time out and stayed with my mum for a couple of months in Spain, but I even ended up doing shows there for an animal shelter charity which then led to copious amounts of reading requests. I just couldn't say no as I was a people pleaser and had a massive fear of rejection and abandonment no doubt echoing from my abusive past during my childhood.

When I got home, I was back in the chaos and had so much catching up to do. The demand for me got so much that I had to employ a PA as I was working all day then trying to answer emails and media requests until the early hours of the morning. My PA Mel was an absolute godsend. I had met her when we worked together at Southend University just after I left the police. She was my anchor and a beautiful soul and kept me in line!

I also developed a passion for ghost hunting and started up public events where we would investigate amazing places. One of my articles in a magazine was seen in Germany which then led to me being invited to work at an Army base in Paderborn. I adored this work which included workshops as well as dems in local venues. It is incredible how spiritual people connect globally as Sabina and Jimmy welcomed me into their home in Germany every time I visited. Jimmy still does my website bless his heart.

In essence, I was working hard and playing hard just like I did when I was in the police. There were never enough hours of the day. This time though, there was a tiny ticking, it was slow and steady and barely audible but as it got louder, I should have listened as it was a time bomb waiting to go off. Ignorant of this impending explosion, I adored every minute of my single life and felt on top of the world as I continued the *Nicky Alan* ride.

The most life-changing spiritual upgrade was when I was taken to a place called The Crystal Palace. I will not go into too much detail here as I describe this place meticulously in my next book. Suffice to say, The Crystal Palace is the source of the Universe. It houses the Archangels, The Reality Layer (Heaven), Spirit Guides, Ascended Masters, The Omnipresence (God), The Akashic Records (Book of Souls) and every celestial being and frequency you could possibly imagine. It is wondrous and infinite and never fails to amaze me with its teachings. It opened up my whole being to a new way of spiritual understanding. I never get tired of meditating and going up to this frequency. I know that so much of my vast knowledge is due to being able to visit this place and then share it with humankind.

Many developing Mediums get in contact with me, thinking there is something wrong because they don't know their guides and I always answer in the same way. This isn't a race; we all develop at our own pace. When guides need to introduce themselves to us properly, they will. When they want to identify themselves with a name, it will happen. If they want to introduce you to a new ability or upgrade, it will be done. It's all about patience. We RECEIVE from the divine, we don't order! (However, when I ask for something, I generally get it!)

I am going to whizz you back in time again to when I had just returned from Hogwarts, the psychic college. I was starting to get used to Catherine being around when I did readings. Sensing that she was with me one day, I put a cheeky request in to her:

'Catherine, it is great that I can now see people's bodies, their souls and their future but could I ask to see Spirit people with my own eyes please? Sometimes it gets so jumbled, with all of the visions being in my third eye.'

I didn't get a response or even a sign, so I thought *fair enough*, quite grumpily! About three days later a lovely lady came to me for a reading. Straight away her wonderful husband came through. The frustrating thing was I could feel him, sensed what he wanted to say, but had no visions in my mind at all. I was getting quite frustrated and said to him out loud, 'Come on John, let me see you because I need to describe you, mate!'

I was flabbergasted! This mist started to appear on the wall to my right. John then popped his head in! I was so shocked I think the lady thought I was loopy! I could see every line, wrinkle, scar and hair on his face. It was truly incredible. I was just laughing hysterically as I had been delivered exactly what I had wanted! I could hear him saying, 'I don't know what you are laughing at, you asked for it!' It made for great evidential readings, being able to view and describe such intricate details. You will always see me now, when I work, looking to my right as that is where I receive my visual information.

In the immediate aftermath I went back to seeing people in my mind's eye and thought it had just been one lucky event. It was about two weeks later; I was doing an intimate afternoon in a pub room in Kent. I knew some of the lovely people there, which made for a very fun and high energy afternoon. However, one of the girls in the group I had never seen before. I started to bring her brother through from the Spirit World. I looked rather impatiently at the stain glassed window as I thought that someone was peeking in through it, being nosey. I was so wrong! A man walked through smiling and stood there holding a pint and a cigarette. He was huge!

I described him to a tee, causing everyone to recognise him instantly. It must have helped as the pub was a regular haunt for him (pardon the pun!), so he found it easy to manifest there.

From that day on, if I asked them to materialise to help the connection, they would around 90% of the time. I felt so lucky. I also learned about temporary spirit guide upgrades. I recall seeing a Japanese man who came to me in a meditation. He took my hand and led me onto this magnificent bridge. On the apex of the bridge, he stopped and showed me all of the golden Koi carp swimming in the water below. He said to me that I must think about the fish. It swims contentedly, remains focused on its path and never bumps into any of his fellow fish, representing community and peace. 'He is sustained in the water and has everything he needs,' he said. He then showed one swimming up a waterfall which he said represented tenacity, bravery and fortitude. He then went on to describe them as adaptable and that I must always adapt to obstacles that cross my path. He said that wealth was represented in the Koi but not to abuse that wealth and to invest wisely.

He was so knowledgeable. It was a wonderful experience and it gave me a lot of life lessons. I saw him a couple of times more, for him to remind me the way of the Koi but I haven't seen him since. This also happened with a woman from Tibet who just popped into a meditation. She came and told me about enduring life through spiritual, emotional and physical pain. I had no idea at the time what she meant as, personally, I felt fine. I now know she was referring to my catastrophic accident that I talk about in my first book, *M.E. Myself and I: Diary of a Psychic*. I knew that she was from Tibet when she pointed to her tent-like structure and said, 'Drokpa'. As soon as the meditation ended, I googled it and a dropka is a black tent that their nomads live in. I do love it when they give me something that I can confirm as being true when I check it!

Another time a darling elemental who looked like the actor Leonardo DiCaprio as a goblin in the film *Lord of the Rings* came into my mind when I was in the bath. He had amazing green eyes, pointy ears and was very small in stature, a typical elemental. I felt myself get lost in a wonderful dimension full of crystals and waterfalls. The elemental guide showed me a clear crystal in his hand shining prisms of light. (This is where my Prism Living Course came from!) He said to me,

'Always adhere to the purity of a crystal. Always remember the four TR's to stay on your spiritual path.

TRust the Spirit World implicitly and the messages you get from them

TRansparency must be in your energy and ego at all times

TRuth everything will always be successful if you say your truth and if you adhere to all of the above it will lead to…

TRansition the next stage of your learning will come to pass.'

All of my past students will smile if they read this. I taught everyone this concept, the four TR's. I never saw that lovely man again.

The answer to a Medium's question: 'How do I develop my ability?' is simply to meditate! The more you do it the more you are connected-up, ready to get the information that you need to progress your spiritual journey!

The next upgrade was a little daunting, as I felt like I was going back in time to a Victorian parlour séance! I decided to do a trance session and let Julianus come and have a talk with my students. I literally felt myself disappear from my own body. It was like I was sitting in a room far away and could only just make out what was being said by Julianus. I had never gone this deep before but trusted the process and Julianus. When I came out of the trance I was faced with many gawping mouths and wide eyes. At the bottom of my feet was this residue. It looked a little like gloopy, clear slime. One of my students actually tasted it and said that it was very salty. It had to be ectoplasm as there was no other explanation as to why this was under my bare feet. Some of the students had also seen me breathe out a white mist whilst Julianus was talking, another first stage of ectoplasmic mist. This indeed was physical Mediumship at its beginnings. From then on, I would sit weekly with a circle of advanced students for physical Mediumship. We encountered moving objects, smells within the room that everyone experience and independent direct speech. IDS is a phenomenon as mentioned in a previous chapter where Spirits use the ether to create sound, usually their own voice or as close to it as they can.

As we continued the physical circle, we started to regularly get a strong smell of smoke. We then became aware of a little girl who trotted around the circle telling us quite happily that she was going to be our little guardian. She said she was called Emily, adored her patent shoes and came from the Victorian era where she had died in a house fire. She loved to come and visit. Incredibly, I found her again when I went to work at an old stately home in Devon many years later! This had been the house that she had lived in but that's for another book!

All in all, the upgrades came and went. When I started to get very strong on, for example, addresses that the spirit gave me, I used to think, *fab* I can get addresses now but then that ability would disappear, and I wouldn't get them again for a while. It could be surnames, dates, the times they passed, what was with them in the coffin, jobs and other identifying features of the spirit person communicating. As the years went on, it all evened out. I also found that certain spirits can prove better at sending across some things more than others. I discovered it was down to the age of their soul, their personality, how long they had been up and how many times that they had blended with a Medium. Some wouldn't shut up talking, others it was like getting blood from a stone.

Spirit people can sometimes get frustrated with their human loved ones. I think a lot of clients come to Mediums expecting us to talk to their loved ones clearly and give them everything they expect. This is so wrong! We can't order who comes through. We can't guarantee that everything the sitter wants to know will be answered. We just have to accept whatever we receive and everyone should be grateful that we have got some form of contact and proof from someone that has passed. Truth be told, the longer I worked for my celestial bosses, the more I got frustrated with human expectation and ego! For instance, you would bring their sister in but all they wanted was their mum and would be demanding things like why she hadn't come through, why hadn't she mentioned the new baby, the divorce etc. Why, why, why! The best one was and still is, 'That can't be them, they wouldn't have known that they were already dead!' For some reason humans think that Spirit people know nothing else after they pass, of course they do! They watch you every day if they wish to, and they will know about all events that take place after their death. They can go everywhere, and see and hear everything, whether you are aware of them or not.

Word to the sitters, leave your egos, expectations and orders of who you want to hear from at the door, relax and you will experience a spectacular reading. I love it and laugh when someone comes in and answers no to everything you say until they get who they come for! I won't entertain it to be honest. I call them out and tell them not to be so rude, if Aunt Nelly wants to come in before your dad to say hello, then say hello to her first!

As my granddad always used to comment, 'The only bad part of this job is that you have to work with the living!' On the whole, I have to admit, 99% of the thousands of people that I have given readings for have been amazing. Always bear in mind that the more open, relaxed and communicative you are with a Medium, the better quality of reading you shall get. We aim for the perfection of a triangular energy. You, me and the spirit communicator, when all are equal, it works spectacularly. It is true when we say we are only as good as our audience!

The other upgrade which proved frustrating was being connected to the energy of the Universal Spikes that took place. For instance, I would dream of being near a volcano and running away from the lava. Within 48 hours a huge volcano would erupt. I would wake up crying for no reason, only to discover that a major figure had died, and I soon realised that I was picking up on the human emotion lacing through the world. Days like Princess Diana dying, Michael Jackson, the Queen, all make for empaths and psychics to feel awfully depressed and unmotivated. I dreamt of 9/11 days before it happened, the civil riots in the UK in 2011, Hurricane Catrina, to name a few; I would have a sense of impending doom and see flashes of fire, anger, fear and rage. It is frustrating, as you know something is coming but what can you do? Who will listen? I have had so many people email me from all over the world or contact me on social media saying they have prophetic dreams but what's the point as nobody will listen? I always explain that it is part of being an empath and an intuitive, it means that your energy pulses with the Universe and feels every spike in energy that takes place. We can basically feel the Geiger counter of the planet.

As I shared in an earlier chapter, I did call the police when I saw murders before and after they had happened in dreams, but I was never really taken seriously. The fact I have relayed the information seems to sate the spirit victims that come to me, so they must assume that I have done everything that I can. As mentioned with the Suffolk murders, the victims find a way to bring their family to me so they can achieve some form of peace both down here and up there.

The next upgrade I had on a huge scale was one of the best in my opinion. It came as a shock initially but as I am an animal lover, it has proven the most precious one of all. I was on holiday in Florida and I had booked a trip through the Everglades. When I came off the boat, there was a horse sanctuary on the grounds by the quay. I felt compelled to go there and asked if I could stroke the horses. She agreed that I could go into the paddock. There were horses of all different shapes and sizes, along with some goats, pygmy goats, chickens, ducks and geese. It was delightful.

I then saw a horse that was standing away from all the rest and I knew I had to approach him, something I did from the front so as not to surprise him in any way. I walked slowly, allowing him to see my every move. I gently whispered to him comforting words and then started stroking his nose, his face and ears. When I reached my arms down his neck, I found myself hugging him for a very long time.

He then jerked his head up and started to back away.

'I cannot believe you are hugging that horse!' said the girl in charge of the sanctuary. The horse became unsettled and continued to move away from me, snorting.

I said without even thinking, 'You mustn't approach him from behind darling, that is what is upsetting him. The man would jump towards him from behind and beat him, he remembers that trauma. Never approach from behind or to the side, he needs to see you and know what moves you are going to make.'

'Oh my God, how did you know that he was beaten?'

I just blurted out, 'He told me.' I reddened as I thought she was going to kick this English nutter out who proclaimed to be the next Doctor Doolittle!

'Oh my, you are a horse whisperer!' she said with a huge smile.

'Well, not quite.' I felt relieved she was open to it and perhaps an empath. 'I didn't know that I had it in me, to be fair, but I am telling you always approach him from the front and you will be fine.'

I then started to mention things that had happened in the last couple of days at the sanctuary. I ended up having the whole staff there who delighted in what I was saying. They confirmed he had been beaten and that he would suddenly buck and rear as they got near, and they didn't know why. I showed them how to approach this beautiful horse and I know I left him feeling so much happier. I would give anything to go back to that place to see how he is getting on.

I am not saying that I can talk to animals, but they have a soul. That soul communicates emotions whether they are good or bad, and that day marked my welcomed ability to sense animals and receive visions, thoughts and feelings from them. I could sense animals' energies, their moods and know if they were hurting, suffering, happy or sad. It was truly an amazing upgrade and I wouldn't swap it for the world!

Animal. Magic!

CHAPTER 18

Pet Heaven

———— ★ ★ ★ ————

Second to losing a loved one is losing our pets. In fact, I've found that some people were more upset over losing a pet than a family member! I know that our fur-babies are like our children so I was interested to see how my Mediumship would develop on blending with animals' souls.

I've had a lot of chats with Julianus about the subject because I wanted clarity on which animals have souls and those who don't. I asked does a bee have a soul? I received a very complicated answer. When we talk about livestock, I was told that yes, they do have a soul but they haven't got a conscious connection to it. Even though they can experience various emotions they are not aware of a higher power or any connection that resonates with humans, unless they experience the love between a human and them. When there is a love connection the soul seems to get stimulated by this connection. So, for instance, a cow that is saved and looked after by a human as a pet, they seem to develop an awareness of love and sentience. As I said, it is complicated and I don't think I will ever get the full answer until I am back home in the Spirit World. However, there seems to be a spiritual evolvement in animal souls where they ascend to levels of higher intelligence and sensory awareness with each incarnation.

So, the cows that become pets are ascended higher and have had many more lifetimes than, say, a cow bred purely to provide beef. On which note, I should point out that this subject makes me cringe when thinking of animals as being live food! Through their incarnations they have gathered wisdom and knowledge of earth that allows them to develop empathy, love and 'human' connections with their owners and humankind. They ascend differently to human energy, we choose harder experiences with each incarnation, they receive easier, less traumatic ones. There seems to be a smudge of a soul in every living being that is taken back up to the Spirit World, they just don't have the conscious connection to it. So, an ant is matter and is connected to the universal energy, just as a whale is but it appears they do not consciously connect with their soul. I hope this explanation makes sense.

They all have intelligence; they all have emotions and feelings but their spiritual awareness is nil until their soul ascends and wants to connect with humans and join them on a more intimate level. I think that is all I can cover on this subject as I have spent many years asking the same question about animals and I always get the same answer.

Dogs, cats and domestic animals are evolved souls incarnated into animals that are there to bring us unconditional love and support during our incarnation. They are, as far as I am concerned, Earth Angels. They are here for just a little while as they deserve to go back to Heaven without having to endure a whole life of heavy human energy. They expect to be loved and constantly crave to make connections with us. And yet we let down the animal kingdom all over the planet. I could be in danger of getting on my soapbox here, so I will leave it by simply saying that all of the animal and planet abusers will receive their karma when up in the Spirit World! For the record I hope the animal souls are near and watch it as it happens!

Animals can read our energy, they can connect with us on a telekinetic level, hence why many psychics can blend with an animal and sense their feelings and physical condition. Animal Reiki is such a powerful practice. Animals don't understand placebos or what is happening so their raw reaction to the healing is mind-blowing. My friend Lindsey frequently visits an animal shelter, to be with the animals. She is an animal Reiki healer and is formidable. There was a dog there that was so tense and stressed it was literally throwing itself at the wall and doing back flips. He would not rest and all the other dogs barking made him worse. Within twenty minutes of Lindsey getting her hands on him, he was sound asleep and completely relaxed, oblivious to his surroundings. He got rehomed very swiftly because of his calm temperament which I feel if someone saw how stressed he was before, they would have walked past him.

It was quite early on after becoming a full time Medium that I realised the importance of connecting with animals in the Spirit World. A lovely man had come for a reading with me and, although I picked up a lot of his family in the Spirit World, I sensed I hadn't got the nugget, the reason he had come to see me. I covered his life and his husband and what had been happening but still I sensed the anticipation of something I had yet to uncover. A couple of times I had seen a horse in my visions, but I put this down to his partner liking to have a little bet every now and then. It was a learning curve and I wish I had mentioned it sooner.

The horse came back into my head. He was a chestnut colour and had a gleaming coat. I saw 16.2 and knew this meant his height. I saw the word, *Dobbin* which I thought was hilarious. I said to the man, 'Okay this is either going to be amazing or totally embarrassing but I can see this chestnut horse, he is 16.2 hands and I can see the name Dobbin?'

The man slid onto the floor crying his eyes out.

'My husband nicknamed him Dobbin, he said that he was a plodder! Oh, my baby, my baby is okay.'

He then rocked himself on the floor knowing that his horse, his darling fur-child who he had raised from a foal was okay. I sensed that the horse had died of a twisted gut and came up with his name, Brandy. That was all this man needed. I realised that he had travelled a long way down the country just to hear that his horse was well. After that day I no longer took animal connections lightly.

To me, animals bring the most joy and I view them as my Earth Angels keeping me going, keeping me company, loving me unconditionally and de-stressing me with their cuddles. As a child I adored the book, *The Lion, The Witch and The Wardrobe*, I would love animals to rule over humans!

It was no surprise that when my fur-baby Meena passed, I was inconsolable. I had managed to heal a tumour in her throat with holy water and a Selenite wand. The oncology department at Cambridge University were completely taken aback when the scan of her neck showed it completely clear, devoid of the tumour that had been in the process of killing her. They recorded it as an anomaly. I still had that sinking feeling however when the vet called me to say that the tumour had disappeared. I had asked the Spirit World years before to tell me when Meena would pass, given the prospect of which had been terrifying me all of the time. She had kept me company through my police retirement and breakdown, and to lose her would be catastrophic. Angels told me that 13 was her number. I assumed it was 13 years old, so I relaxed. The thing was when I first went up to the Oncology Department at Cambridge it was the 13th August. We had used the A1301 road to get there and, amazingly, her patient number also had 13 in it. I knew then that she was going to go.

It turned out that I had missed the tumour growing in her belly. It was my birthday on the 17th September and Meena was moving very slowly, her tummy had become huge. I knew that she had stayed with me for my birthday, so on the 20th I slept with her on the sofa-bed downstairs and I whispered in her ear, 'Darling, I know you waited for my birthday but I really mean this, it is time for you to go home now, I will be okay. Just go home as you are tired and I don't want you to suffer anymore. Tomorrow, when we go and see the vet man, just let go my darling and I will see you one day again when I come home too.'

I nuzzled into her as she let out a little cry. I was sobbing the whole night as I knew she was going home the following day. She was only eight and I was devastated. Sure enough, they put her to sleep on the table as they had never seen such a huge and fast-growing tumour in their life. As I sat outside sobbing my heart out my phone went. My friend who was a Medium said my dad had just come to her and said that Meena had just passed and that she would keep me company in the early days by showing me rainbows because that's where she was at the Rainbow Bridge. I didn't give a shit she was at the Rainbow Bridge, I wanted her here!

The Rainbow Bridge is what is known as Pet Heaven. I have seen it many times now. For some reason animals seem to go through an energy portal in Heaven that looks like a huge prism. Perhaps it is their version of the life review we get by Archangel Jeremiel when we go up. After the prism light clears, I then see them running around like nutters, healthy and very happy with their spirit family.

I just wanted my baby girl back and was in total misery. Unfortunately, two days later I had to do a retreat in Scotland. Thankfully most of the people knew me so if I burst into tears they understood. The first day up there, a huge rainbow shone over the hotel and the surrounding moors. I was bitter that my baby girl had been taken so I put the rainbow down to being in the Highlands and the climate there causing rainbows to be common. However, this took place every single day. Wherever we were there was a rainbow. My students would eagerly spot them and show them to me every time they flashed across the sky. There was a magnificent one that ended right in the middle of a loch!

I can't express my thanks and gratitude to those magnificent people as they helped me through the whole retreat. Perhaps Meena had timed it that way. When I got home it didn't stop there. I had a nail appointment and, as I was talking to the technician, I said about seeing rainbows every day. She smiled and lifted her top, 'I had this done last week as it was my nan's favourite song and she has just died.'

There on her ribs was a rainbow with the words, 'Somewhere Over the Rainbow'. I couldn't believe what I was seeing. When I got back in the car, Eva Cassidy came on singing the exact same song, backing up the signs I had already seen. The following day I was headlining at the Mind Body and Spirit Exhibition at Olympia in London. I really didn't want to go but knew I had to. I was on the train wondering what sort of thing I would see today and in that moment a man opposite me leant forward. Inside his collar were the colours of the rainbow! The following day I was given a packet of tissues at Olympia to give to someone in the audience who was crying from a message I was giving them. They were Andie tissues, and if you are familiar with the brand, you'll know what is on the logo…

This continued day after day, I couldn't believe it. I wasn't looking out for rainbows; they were put right in front of me.

I had to go up to Cambridge to pick up Meena's ashes. I took them outside and sat under a sycamore tree. I looked up to the sky and a rainbow formed, I was so happy to see it as I was crying my heart out. I then heard a tap on her wooden box and a sycamore seed had landed on it, the ones people often refer to as helicopters because of the way they spin when they fall. I kept it with me for the way home. I had to get some petrol on the way and, as I stepped onto the garage forecourt, my foot walked into a huge pile of sycamore seedlings. Over the years this has always been a sign from Meena as well, in fact I currently have one on my bedside cabinet that landed on my head six days ago, the day that she passed, 21st September!

The following week I had to do some shows in Hampshire. I was in Gosport checking out the hall, when I had to stop to take a call. As I looked to my right there was a shop called Rainbow's End. I knew then I'd had my grieving time with the rainbow signs. After that I no longer saw them every day. That night I did my usual thing before a public show of Mediumship, I sat quietly for a while and sent a thought up that I was about to work. I then visualised the Spirit World coming down to me and us meeting together so that I could start to get messages from the Spirit people in the queue. It didn't happen initially, instead my dad came up to me and smiled in my mind. He whistled and Meena came trotting up to him and nudged the side of my dad's leg. I started to cry, my dad winked and said, 'It's okay, I have her now.'

It was so magical. In fact, a couple of years later a Medium described my dad and said that he was whistling. She then said that a huge red dog was trotting next to him. Meena was a bullmastiff so she had this spot on! It was just another bit of wonderful proof that my dad was looking after Meena. The last time I went up to see my family she was snoring and had her head on my dad's feet! Bless her heart!

I gained Teddy, my next dog, unexpectedly on the 31st March the following year. He had been left abandoned and I needed to rescue him. I felt guilty as I was still grieving Meena. I got something through the post the next week and it was a follower who had drawn Meena and next to her was a rainbow. She had also attached a sycamore seedling to the card, I could not believe it. I was even more shocked when I saw the date that she had drawn the picture, it was the 31st March. It was Meena giving her blessing, I am sure of it. I asked that beautiful lady why she had decided to paint the picture and send the sycamore seed on that particular day. She said that she just felt an urgent need to do it. She said that she had no idea why she had to send a sycamore seed, she just knew that she had to enclose it with the picture. How magnificent is that?

Just for the record, I do feel that our pets in our soul clusters can reincarnate into another dog during our human life. It cannot be done with humans but I know that Pepper, a rough collie, my second family dog was so like Meena it was unbelievable even down to the fact that both of them sat with their hind legs and bums on the sofa with their front legs on the floor! It is the same with my Mia now. She is so much like my boxer Jasper, even though she is a Shih

Tzu. She sleeps like him; she has accidents all the time like him and every now and then her mannerisms send a shiver down my spine. I know that our guardian fur-babies come down to help us through the worst times of our lives. They are our lifeline, I believe, to keep us contented and loved down here. I just wish the planet respected animals more and respected how intelligent and magnificent every species really is.

So, know that your loving pets, no matter what shape, size and species, will be there waiting for you just like your family and friends are. In the meantime, they may send you a sign, you may feel them brush past you or land on your bed when they come to visit. All in all, they remain with you for eternity and that gives me so much comfort.

Animals. Forever x

CHAPTER 19

We Are Not Dead Yet!

———— ★ ★ ★ ————

I was forever learning from my celestial bosses during my Mediumship dems, private readings and workshops. I was faced once with such a huge quandary; I ended up silent on the rostrum not knowing what to say.

I was doing a special Evening of Mediumship at Walthamstow in London. The place was absolutely packed. I recall this beautiful boy who came to me called Sam. All I could see was that he was lying in bed with lots of tubes connected to him. The first thing he said to me was, 'Can you tell my nan to change the station to music I love, I hate that classical rubbish!'

I thought this was odd as he was saying these words in the present tense. In my mind I suddenly saw Sam being stabbed in the head, he was in a coma and I knew without a doubt he was never going to get well. I could not believe it; I was communicating with someone that was still alive! I put his information out into the room. His brother's girlfriend, Kisha, was in the audience and put her hand up straight away to confirm that indeed Sam was in a coma after being stabbed. It was obvious that she would want to know if he was going to make it but Sam told me he wasn't going to come out of the coma. The reason I stayed silent for so long was that I had no idea whether to tell Kisha that he was never coming back or just let it lie. It was an agonising decision for me.

Sam was there to bring messages to his family about the trial for the people who had stabbed him. I also learned that night your soul can leave its living body and communicate with Mediums. It was ground-breaking stuff to say the least! I had communicated with a man before who said he was in a coma, whom I thought I may have been working on a psychic level, but this connection nailed it for me.

Kisha has kindly provided what she recalled of the evening's message by Sam, which is written out below. The stunning revelations of a beautiful boy in a coma.

Nicky - I'm being guided to this side of the room. I have a young man with me and I feel like I want to make this action.

Nicky pointed to her head around her ear area and made a stabbing motion with her fingers.

Nicky - I feel like this is happening then I'm falling backwards. There's a wall behind me and it's raining.

She kept making the same motion with her fingers.

Mo, my friend, nudged me and said, 'It's you!'

My legs were already shaking, I couldn't believe it could be true.

I raised my hand and Nicky said to me, 'Does the name Anthony mean something to you?'

Kisha - Yes.

Nicky - He's telling me that you're his sister.

Kisha - I'm his brother's girlfriend, but he would call me that, yes.

Nicky - I'm getting a sense that he hasn't fully crossed over or the family haven't accepted that he's gone.

Kisha - He was stabbed in the head. He's in a coma in a vegetative state.

Nicky - This is incredible. This has only ever happened to me once before when...

Nicky then relays a story about when a man in a coma came through, he told his granddaughter's friend to tell her to go see him because he was about to pass away.

Nicky - Is his name Anthony?

Kisha - No it's Sam, Anthony is his cousin who was with him when it happened.

Nicky - He says he doesn't know if he will make it back but he is sending you all lots of love and wants you to know that he knows you are there. He wants to say stop leaving the radio on that awful music, it's driving him mad.

We all laugh.

Nicky asks me and Mo to wait at the end so she can talk to us privately.

We had a lovely conversation where she told me that this had been such an amazing experience, she will write about it in her book.

I told her how awful I felt it was that Sam was stuck in his body but Nicky said he wasn't stuck; his soul was free to move around on the celestial plain.

She told me that she sees sadness in me. She knows I'm unhappy but things will get better.

I put my head in my hands and start to cry.

Nicky - why can I see St Lucia?

Kisha - I'm going there at the end of the month.

Nicky - That's exactly what you need. That trip will be the making of you. When you come back things will be better for you.

A few years later we went back to see Nicky. At the end of the evening, I approached her and asked her if she remembered me. She held both of my hands and said, 'of course I do my darling, it's lovely to see you.'

She told me that she remembered Sam coming through and how special it was for her.

I told her that I had left my boyfriend and as far as I was aware Sam was still the same. She told me that he had said he wouldn't be coming back but she hadn't told me at the time because of how close I was to the family.

Thank you, Kisha for adding such a wonderful addition to my book x

When I started doing readings 32 years ago, I hadn't experienced a family member passing after a long chronic illness, where they had lain month after month waiting to die. So, when I then started to do readings, I questioned if I would prefer to know someone was dying or just find out that they had already died. I still don't know really, the agony of being with someone that you know is going to die is so traumatic because the grieving process is so prolonged. What I have learned from Spirit people over the years is what is actually happening when they are waiting to die. The most common questions I get asked is, 'Did they know I was there? Are they aware that they were dying? Were they scared?'

I got the answer one evening. I was doing a reading for a lovely lady and her two girls in Wickford, Essex. They seemed very upbeat and a joy to work with. Their mum/nan came through and said that her name was June, before proceeding to name every family member she could. She gave lots of evidence that proved it was indeed her talking. What was weird, though, was every time I asked her how she passed she wouldn't answer. Instead, in my mind's eye, I just kept seeing her lying in bed and laughing. She then started to say about the girls visiting her every Wednesday. She said that they normally came Saturdays and Wednesdays but only came on the Wednesday now. She knew how busy they were and wanted to make it clear that she didn't want them coming twice a week because it must be so upsetting and boring for them! This was the cruncher, making me stop in my tracks and think, what the hell?

June said, 'I heard what you said last Wednesday about Brian moving on to another home because of his promotion. Tell him not to worry about me, I will be fine.'

I felt so confused as that statement was in the present. This wasn't a memory or going back to a time when she was alive. As I looked perplexed at the girls, they beamed and in total shock told me that their mum/nan was still alive but in the last stages of severe dementia! I was overwhelmed. Everything she said was correct down to what she was wearing when they visited, their conversations, everything. Incredibly, her soul had visited and blended with mine - she had astral-planed. Her soul had left her body and come to visit me whilst she was still living and breathing.

So that experience has taught me that whatever state your loved ones are in, whether it's a coma, cancer, dementia, they CAN still hear you, they know everything that is going on around them. We are the victims witnessing our loved one's decline, not them; they are just impatient as they just want to go up and experience Heaven again!

I see it as akin to when you come to the end of your holiday. Once you are packed up in preparation to leave, you just want to get home as you know the holiday is over.

June went onto explain that she can go up and visit all of her relatives in spirit whenever she wants and they visit her too. This made me realise that when you go to your senile relative and they state that a dead relative has just visited, take it as fact, as they most probably have just popped in!

I have also lost count of how many times Spirit people have stated who was with them as they were dying, what time it was, who was holding their hands, and what was said to them when they were in an unconscious state. I have received thousands of messages like this so believe me when I say: they may be waiting for their physical body to die but they are totally aware of who is there and what is being said.

They are also aware of Spirit people who are waiting for them to come up or have come down to collect them. Hospice staff refer to this as the death stare. It is when dying people suddenly become lucid and stare into a corner of the room or the ceiling and start mentioning people who have passed over, or they see angels (more than likely Archangel Azrael Archangel who presides over death). It has been recorded time and time again, so please know that your loved ones are never alone. So many people hold guilt that they didn't make it to the passing, please don't feel guilty, they are never alone. They have both living and/or passed family there to comfort them and ease them through their transition. They are also excited to go and catch up with their loved ones and to move on to the next phase. I have never had one spirit person tell me they were scared or alone. I feel that we think they are and imagine the worst in our grief.

I have also had messages from Spirit people who describe you visiting them in the Chapel of Rest. They are more alive than you can imagine. The death of their physical body is the new beginnings of a free, powerful soul that is completely at peace and devoid of any pain; ready to travel to wherever they wish.

Since that occasion I have had many people with dementia come through in this way before they have even passed. I have also been able to communicate with the soul of extremely disabled children and adults that can't speak or communicate in a normal way. I also love blending with severely autistic children, so I can give messages to their parents. This is how Mediums can connect with animals, they have souls, we can communicate with them just as easily as a human.

It is all rather magical if we look at physical death in this way. I always imagine my loved ones flying up to Heaven and rejoicing in their reunion with loved ones (pets most definitely included) rather than picture them alone and dead and in a morgue somewhere. That's how I cope when they pass over.

Picture. Heaven x

CHAPTER 20

Now for the Angels!

———— ★ ★ ★ ————

I can't really profess to knowing and seeing angels from a child, like I saw Spirit people. If you have read my first book, you will know that after bouts of abuse as a young teen, I would rock away on my own and hear in the distance what sounded like females singing or chanting. I never knew what it was and never really had the energy or the curiosity to find out where the music was coming from. I found out many years later what it was and felt so embarrassed at the time! I will explain this in a minute!

I have to say, I knew of angels in my late teens but had never really raised my vibration enough to bother connecting with them or even seeing if I could. To be honest, I was too focused on training and wanting to be a Police Officer. I was however, obsessed with collecting angel and fairy figurines, something I merely put down to taste. I had to have an angel within sight everywhere I went even in the car. I never realised that this is what most Earth Angels do. I don't want to get too deep into Earth Angels but they are a particular soul incarnation who are put on this Earth purely to aid mankind with a little help from the angel realms!

It wasn't until I became a professional full time Medium that they started to gently introduce themselves in the most incredible ways. Naturally, my students adored angels and so the subject came up quite a lot. I was aware that you could invoke certain angels and that they could help us, guide us and warn us of inherent danger. I wasn't too interested as I was passionate about the afterlife, so as a Medium tended to send my energy to the zone of the Spirit World and my guides. There are certain layers that Mediums connect with. We can change our frequency and intent to join with a specific layer. Plains of existence can get a bit complicated but here they are as a quick, basic reference:

Spirit World– Heaven

Spirit Guides

Ascended Masters i.e., Jesus, Mohammed, Buddha

Angels

The Omnipresence – The Source – God.

I am so humbled to say that I now connect with all of these realms but, back in the day, I wasn't too fussed. I used to visit a lovely lady, Jenny, who used to run a spiritual stall in my local indoor market. I bought myself a set of angel cards, *Angels of Light* by Diana Cooper and became intrigued as, every time I used them and asked a question, they always gave me exactly what I needed to know. Thirty years on I still have them and continue to adore them. So, you could say, my subconscious was connecting with the angel realms on a daily basis as I asked them questions via the cards.

It wasn't until I was on my way to do a dem in London that I had my first direct encounter. I was with my friend and because of traffic and a very sore ankle, we were running late. I was storming along the A127 just near Wickford, Essex. This is a two-lane arterial road that leads towards London. I was most probably speeding as usual; I have never been a patient driver! Whilst I was talking to my friend, I suddenly heard a big booming voice say, 'BRAKE, NOW!'

I knew I had to listen and promptly slammed on my brakes in the outside lane of a 70-mph zone. We both shot forward but, luckily, had seatbelts on. It was then I saw a huge tractor wheel bouncing along the road towards us, its diameter taller than the height of my car. It was if it was in slow motion as it bounced right in front of us and then over the central barrier and onto the other side of the dual carriageway where, thank goodness, there was no oncoming traffic. We watched it continue on safely into a field, where it landed rather clumsily, like a giant penny might come to a rest in a ditch after a few spins.

I know without a doubt that if we had kept on driving, the tyre would have smashed into the car, most probably killing us. We both sat there, gob-smacked, unable to believe what had just happened. I could feel myself shaking and realised that something huge had just transpired, saving our lives. We got to the church and I was grateful to have my time in the side room to link up. Straight away my granddad, Fred, was there.

'Hi, what are you doing here granddad?'

'Hi darling. One, you shouldn't really be doing this today as you have sprained your ankle. Two, the angels saved you from a bad accident, you really should talk to them more. And three, don't go over your time to finish just because you turned up late!'

Nice warm and fluffy message from my granddad! Ha! It was true, I had sprained my ankle and I knew that I was breaking one of the Mediumship laws about working when you are ill, exhausted or in pain. I didn't want to let the church down but the lady there was so rude to me when I finally arrived that I never went back anyway! I did try and go over time and deliver a few more messages for the congregation, but all I kept seeing was my granddad shaking his head when I tried to link to another spirit being!

The thing that really made my heart race was the thoughts of how I had managed to avoid the accident with the tractor tyre. I didn't know who it was, how they made such a loud voice boom like that - especially because my friend hadn't heard it - and what would happen next. Was it a one off or was the voice's owner now part of my life? I didn't have long to find out. I started to buy more packs of angel cards and used them daily for guidance, as well as incorporating them in some of the readings I was doing. I loved the thought that I was being guided and watched by angels.

One evening I was at my ex's mum's house in Purley, Surrey. It was late at night and I needed to get back home. As I bent down to put my shoes on, I heard that familiar booming voice saying 'NO'. A huge chill snaked down my back and I knew that I must not get in the car and drive. I told my partner at the time and he respected what I had said, agreeing that we weren't going to drive home.

The following morning, we heard that there had been a huge car crash on the M25 motorway. We would have been on that road at that time the night before. This was the second time that the angel voice had stepped in and potentially saved my life.

I still did not have a direct link to them like I did with the Spirit World, but I started to think about them a lot more. A few months later I was in Sainsbury's when my phone rang. I picked it up and was shocked to hear from a producer that they wanted me to audition for a new series called *Angels* that was to be presented by Gloria Hunniford. I stated that I would let them know because, being truthful, angels weren't my first port of call as a Medium!

Incredibly, as I distractedly rummaged through the fruit and vegetables aisle, a woman came up to me out of the blue and said, 'You are a very special lady. You must share your wisdom with everyone you can. Be brave and do it.'

I was in such shock; I merely stood there and watched her walk away from me. What had just happened? I now know the answer: she was delivering what I call an Earth Angel message. I have received so many in my life. Sensitives/empaths/intuitives are influenced by the angel realms to go and do something or say something life-changing to someone.

The woman in the supermarket certainly changed my life that day. I was 80% convinced that I should do the show but feared it making me look like an idiot. I had done some TV programmes before and most of them were okay. However, one particular dining show, *Come Dine with Me* just took the mickey out of me throughout, portraying me in a completely different light to what really happened. I was the guest Medium for my friend who was doing the cooking. She lived in a very old house so I did a very basic guide to ghost hunting. I then spent all evening until stupid o clock doing readings for the diners. Two of them ended up in tears as I brought cherished loved ones through. None of this was shown, instead some of the guests dismissed me and made unnecessary sarcastic comments and the narrator wasn't much better. As I had no editing rights, they could do what they wanted so TV-land was no longer a huge interest to me. My friend won the prize but I just felt like a prized idiot.

However, that night I was lying in the bath and I sent a thought up to the angel realms asking if they wanted me to do the show. I closed my eyes and then felt a little tickle on my left shoulder.

Incredibly, a small white feather had landed there. I looked for any possible explanation of where that feather may had come from, I had nothing. I took this as a sign and phoned the production company the following day. More of TV land in a future chapter!

Starting the show *Angels* is when the full force of the angel realms came bounding down to guide me, communicate with me and show me their ways. The first angel that I saw in full form was in my hallway. I was having a difficult time and asked for a sign. A man-shaped image about seven foot tall, and with the bluest eyes stood staring down at me. I instantly burst into tears as I felt the love and compassion come from this celestial vision. He was dressed in royal blue robes that fell to his feet. As I studied them, I saw a gleaming sword sitting on his left hip.

'I am Michael, I am here to give you the courage to move forward and leave the past behind.'

That is how the angels started coming to me. They showed up, said their name, the colour of their ray and told me how they would help me. I didn't read up on them or study what they did for humankind. I waited patiently until each one introduced themselves and would then relay this to the students and sitters of mine who needed the angels in their lives. I also started to regularly visit the Crystal Palace and learn from them in that frequency.

It was a glorious upgrade and now I can't imagine existing without them being there in the distance, always ready to help when I need them. They are a huge presence and very commanding, portraying a far stronger and more resolute energy compared to spirit guides and Spirit people. They leave you breathless and simply amazed by what they can do to help. You have to experience it for yourself because no one really believes you until they have had the true power of the angels revealing themselves, showing the full force of what they can do. They have provided me with money when I need it, have healed me, have guided me in difficult choices and, perhaps most usefully, always get me a parking space when I need it!

I recall when I was on my way to Wales to do a paranormal investigation. We were on the M4 and suddenly my car completely cut out in the outside lane. I was terrified as it was a busy time of day and I was without any power steering as I tried to guide the car towards the inner lanes. How we didn't get hit by another vehicle, I really don't know.

I screamed 'Archangel Raphael (archangel of healing and safe travel), I need you now! Please come and bring us to safety!'

It was like a miracle. The engine turned on and I managed to get the car up a nearby slipway. Once safe it then completely died on me again. I couldn't believe my eyes when I saw a garage only 100 metres down the road. The kindly man there towed me the last few hundred yards. I explained what happened and he said that my engine computer had completely failed and that it was impossible for the car to start up again after it had died. I looked at my friend and just smiled.

Now, I have to come back to those singing voices I heard in my teens. I was doing an angel workshop in Devon. I took my students up to the Crystal Palace, the home of the angels in meditation, and left them at the main foyer so they could be taken where they needed to go. I found myself in an amazing garden flanked by roses of all colours. There were butterflies and dragonflies swooping around me as I spied a huge fountain and felt drawn to walk to it. I could hear a familiar song that I had not heard for many years. I saw black haired ladies in long ivory Grecian-type robes pouring translucent water over the heads of what looked like suffering humans. They were singing the sweetest song as they bathed these people. Some souls were just normal humans, some were soldiers and some were animals. They then invited me over and sang to me as they poured water over me that they were scooping up from a three-tiered fountain. I knew that it was the Fountain of Life as I had seen it before in another meditation. They made me feel in complete bliss and I asked them who they were.

'We are The Seraphim. This is our garden, welcome.'

That's all they said, and their smiles melted my soul. The love, compassion and peace that emanated from them is something I just can't put into words. They all sang together as I remained in their care, being immersed in a water-like liquid that shone with blues, silvers, greens and turquoises. I was aware after a while that I needed to bring myself back, as I had a whole classroom full of students, but it was hard to draw away from these magnificent beings. As we came back, the first thing I said to my class was, 'Does anyone know what Seraphim means?'

How embarrassed was I? I was supposed to be the tutor and students answered back, 'Yes, they are healing angels for traumatised souls. They heal from the Celestial Garden!' As if they were talking about the weather! That, ladies and gents, is how I found out about the Seraphim! I regressed in time and started to cry in front of everyone as I recognised their song and realised that they had been there with me during the most horrific time of my life, singing away as I rocked myself in my adolescence.

I have subsequently blended with them on many occasions and have learned a lot more about the Seraphim. They dawn new worlds with Mother Gaia and Archangel Ariel. They are also warriors and are the oldest hierarchy of angels that exist. They are fearsome when they need to protect the world and come down in their droves to rescue mass souls when natural disasters or wars take place sporting four faces for East, North, West and South. They are incredible and I don't think there is ever a day that I do not acknowledge them in my thoughts and prayers.

I could literally write a whole book on my angel experiences. In fact, I think I will to prevent this chapter from running on and on!

Invoking angels is easy. Research what angel you need for whatever your challenge is and just ask them to come and help you. You can do this out loud or write it down instead but they need permission to step in and assist you. If you want to heighten your connection, try angel-guided meditations and get a Selenite crystal, also known as the Angel Stone. After you have invoked an angel, you will get a sign that they have heard your plea, usually within a couple of days. Normally it will be a feather, but they can deliver it in all different ways. All I can say is that you will know it when you see it!

Love. Angels.

CHAPTER 21

Is Anybody There?

———— ★ ★ ★ ————

It is as natural as breathing to me to blend with, and feel the presence of, a spirit person. It is something I have taken for granted since I was nine years old. Every single day I get messages and emails from people all over the world wanting to know how they can identify if their loved ones have brought them a sign. It never occurred to me that people do not know what to look for. So, I thought it best if I shared with you how to tell when your loved one comes visiting or is nearby! So many people report to me that they have never had a sign from their loved one. When I take them through all of the possible ways this might be achieved, they realise that they have been visited all along!

Spirit visitation is something I get asked about a lot, merely because it is something that invades our personal lives, our homes and our families if you are getting things that go bang in the night! Ninety-nine per cent of spirit visitors are your family or friends who have passed to the Spirit World and have popped in to say hello.

From my point of view, the main reason for their visits is usually an important time of year for you or them, i.e., their birthday or the anniversary of their passing. This is normally because the whole family unconsciously send thoughts up as a mass energy to that individual. This will be sensed by the person in question and they will come down to be with us to help us get through this difficult time. Christmas is also very popular for spirit visitation. You will always have your spirit loved ones visit for big events, i.e., birthdays, weddings, anniversaries and child births because they want to celebrate with you. Also, if you are finding life tough, can't deal with your grieving, or your health is suffering, they will be down here like a shot. I also hear the lovely stories from my spirit communicators, who might just sit with you, watch you, sleep next to you; purely to keep their soul mate or loved one company. They come down for landmarks in your life even if it's a new job, so it's not just when you are sad or celebrating.

Whether you know it or not, they are with you when you need them. The fact you can't see or hear them is irrelevant, this part has to be based on trust and faith. To me it's extremely simple to spot a visitation, but unless you know what to look for it can appear complicated. So many Spirit people tell me during a reading what their loved one has spoken about that day, what they did yesterday, what they bought in the shops recently, or perhaps describe a newly decorated room in their house. They see everything, hear our thoughts and feel our energy. What I will say at this juncture, as this is another common question, is they do not interfere with our privacy or intimate times! There are certain things that happen that they will not see at all. Think of it this way, why would they want to?

I had to laugh when I did an intimate evening a while ago. A mum had come through to her two daughters. She kept saying the name Jane to them. They couldn't understand the reference.

Their mum then said, 'You should know her, you were moaning about her on the way here!'

Both girls then screamed in shock, they had indeed been gossiping about this particular girl and had said for a laugh whilst driving to come and see me, 'Well mum, if you are really here, tell us about who we have just been moaning about!'

Fantastic! So, they do give evidence of the mundane things in your life, proving they are with you. Lots of them even come to work with you!

The unfortunate thing that harms spirit visitation is the media. I get annoyed by the programmes and films that make visitation by the Spirit World both scary and dangerous. As soon as people encounter anything unusual in their house, they immediately think it's haunted or they have a poltergeist visiting. What nonsense!

Let us just get this bit out of the way. There are a small number of spirit beings who are not friends or family that are connected to your house or like to visit your children. They either passed away there beforehand or have popped in from a neighbour's house and are attracted to your energy. They are harmless and co-exist with you.

Then there are the unwelcome low energy spirit visitors that are exceptionally rare. If you have any of these signs then you are being visited by a not-so-nice entity.

Bad smells (like rotten eggs or sulphur)

Arguments in the house

Depression in the house

Repeated accidents happening

Electrical items failing or blowing up

Physical marks on your body which are totally inexplicable

Plants dying in and around the house

Feeling threatened in your home

If you have any of these signs then seek a reputable Medium or a clergyman.

As I said, these are very rare so let us focus back on our gorgeous Spirit people who visit from Heaven. As a Medium, when I carry out my demonstrations and readings, my energy needs to be in a heightened position. I have to be exceptionally positive, as the vibrations of the Spirit World are so great and pure that if I can't meet them halfway, it's not going to work.

I recently carried out a reading for a lady who wouldn't celebrate her first Christmas without her mum. Her mum came through to say she was so upset that her daughter had experienced such a miserable festive period, not even putting the tree up. She said that if there had been more fun, laughter and light energy, she would have found it so much easier to sit in that energy with her daughter. She still visited, but her daughter was so down she didn't acknowledge or feel her presence, choosing instead to sit in her bedroom with a bottle of wine and cry. Her sister, though, placed a seat at the dinner table for her mum, and she and her children toasted her, using the day as a celebration of her life. The mum found it so much easier to stay in the positive energy. You can see which sister coped without their mum the best that Christmas! Whilst I was blending with the mum she kept saying, 'Please enjoy Christmas in the future. I feel so guilty sometimes seeing you so sad, I didn't mean to pass on Christmas Eve!'

This does not mean to say that you can't grieve, this is just an example of how a spirit person sees and gauges our energy. So, be positive, talk to them out loud with your problems and your thoughts; ask for their help on something. It is always best to talk to a favourite photo of theirs. I do this every time I have a problem, or if I'm happy and just want to send my love. You can also spray their perfume or hold a piece of their clothing to feel more connected to them. Every night I light candles that correspond to a certain loved one and send a thought up to them. I also have a cutting of a Yucca plant that I yanked from my mum's garden as we left for the final time after clearing her home out. That plant now stands six foot tall as it is simply huge! I sometimes sit by the plant in the garden and have a chat with her. I also on occasion say at night, 'Oi mum and dad, I've not heard from you in a while, so make the effort and bring me a sign!' They will always then deliver something in the next 48 hours.

In fact, I have to add this as I am writing. Two nights ago, I did just that, asked where my mum and dad were and why I hadn't heard from them recently. The following night the fire alarm went off at 3am for no reason at all! In the kitchen and lounge there was a weird white mist that initially I thought was smoke but when I realised that nothing was on fire, put it down to ectoplasmic mist.

So, what happens after you have spoken to them? Look for the signs! To feel spirit energy there are a number of ways your body can detect it. Firstly, you may experience a tingling or 'rushing sensation' over your head, like you are being tickled. You may feel goose bumpy or the hairs on the back of your neck will stand up. You may feel either a cold spot or hot area in your house, depending on their energy. Some people get a heat rash around their neck and chest area, but you may also feel breathless or have heart palpitations when they blend with you or if they are standing very close to your energy. A tickly nose is also another sign they are near.

They can also manifest in different stages, where you may see white or black shadows moving out of the corner of your eye. I see a lot of these shadows pass across my hallway; I always shout out a hello to them as I catch them walking past! Sparkling lights is another favourite, going across a room, up the walls, or when it looks like there is rain in the air. You may see orbs as small as a dot to ones as large as a tennis ball, either with the naked eye or in photographs. Orbs are the first stage of a spirit manifesting themselves. They are easily picked up on digital cameras as the electromagnetic field seems to be detected by digital equipment. Don't mistake them for dust particles or insects. Proper orbs normally create their own light source or have a complete luminous halo around them. They can also be seen as rods of light and can be any colour. This is the second stage of spirit manifestation. Please look at your photos carefully and see if any reflective surface could be responsible. If not, then it could be your loved one!

Another favourite sign is the third stage of spirit manifestation, which appears like a white or pale-blue mist, similar to cigarette smoke like we saw the other night after the fire alarm went off. This is known as ectoplasmic mist. So, if you were smoking whilst taking the picture, don't get too excited! Sometimes people actually have a fully manifested face in the orbs or mist, so you know who it is posing for the picture.

The fourth stage of manifestation is when the mist solidifies into a human shape. These are quite popular and are normally seen out of the corner of your eye. They can be any colour and sometimes will look like a passing shadow.

The fifth stage of manifestation is your loved one appearing as solid as you like. They always seem happy and extremely well. I have known many people to come through looking a lot younger and slimmer than when they were about to pass. I certainly will project an image a few pounds lighter! They never look ill or dead, so please don't lay under your duvet fearing they will loom over you like a ghoul! They will never scare you, I promise, as they know what you can handle. I personally ban any Spirit people in my bedroom unless it is urgent or I really need support.

The next phenomenon to look out for is when objects are being apported into your home or around you. This is where your spirit loved ones bring things and put them in weird places that you will notice. The most common are white feathers, they appear in the most obscure places and are pure white and of fluffy appearance. These can also be gifts from your guardian angel or from the angel realms. It depends if you have invoked the angels for assistance or not. Another favourite is coins, always note the date of the coin, it could be relevant.

I was driving home once from a demonstration in Kent. I was sending thoughts up to my dad and felt something hit my lap. In the darkness I could see it was a coin. When I got home, the coin was dated 1980, the year my dad died!

Another example was when a lady came to me as she kept finding dollar bills and American coins in her daughter's cot, as well as around the house. Her dad came through to me to tell her that they were from him as he was American!

Buttons are also brought through as well; you will find that they will not fit or match any of your clothing in the house. Remember though, see if the area they are found in is explainable. The most amazing house I ever visited for this phenomenon was a lady who kept getting nappies put on her landing. She had no babies or such items in the house. She thought she was going mad. I found out on arrival that her spirit baby son was trying to get her attention, and boy did that work! As soon as he had been acknowledged by his mum, the nappies stopped appearing.

Keep all the objects you find in a pot to create a hub of positive energy. I do this and sometimes, when I need a boost, I open the lid to my special pot and almost breathe in the celestial energy that surrounds these apports.

Spirit people can also create a phenomenon where they asport items. This is where objects are taken away and either go missing for good or are moved into another area of the house. My mum found her plastic lottery balls in the oven after they had been missing for days. My spirit nan told me she put them there because my mum had forgotten to say happy birthday to her! I have had someone report that their spirit nan's photograph was in the fridge on the anniversary of their nan's birthday! Figure that one out. Favourites to disappear are keys, remote controls (my remote went missing and never returned!) and especially jewellery. Spirit children love grabbing their mum's jewellery and moving it elsewhere. They also like hairbrushes and combs, anything that their mum will use on a daily basis and will notice when it is missing. Children's toys are another popular pick, they start up on their own or get moved by a spirit sibling.

If something gets lost, ask them out loud to return it. I guarantee it will turn up in an obvious place, one you have already checked before! I had this with my nan's wedding ring. She said she was keeping it for a while as my mum was going to be ill (breast cancer) and when she was better, she would return it. I found it under a huge solid chest of drawers after my mum got the green light! I have no idea how they do it, I just accept that they can!

Look out for repeated numbers as well. Angel numbers can be shown to you they are normally in three's 333, 111, 555. However, Spirit people can do this as well so look out for it. My number from my lot is 7 and 1111, I see it everywhere when they are near. Also, they will occur on license plates on the car in front, showing you a number you recognise or even your loved one's initials or name. In one day, I saw 111 on a dustbin when I was stopped in a traffic queue, I had 111 likes on a TikTok video when I opened the app, I was on stage 111 of my video game, and when my oven bleeped for no reason, the time was 11.10 pm!

Don't forget, they can also bring smells. Remember the cheese man? I have also tasted gravy, all brands of drinks, blood, fruit, candy, chocolate - you name it, I have tasted it! Cigarette smoke is another favourite if they were a smoker, also their favourite aftershave/perfume is quite common. Beer is another good one if your loved one liked a drink or whatever their favourite tipple was. Anything that they know you will recognise as belonging to them, they will bring you. The traditional smell that most people talk about is flowers. They can even create the smell of one particular flower they loved. I normally only smell a strong smell of flowers when I have cleared a home or a space with my guides and angels.

Your loved ones can manifest sound so you may hear your name being mentioned any time during the day or night. A lot of people report hearing it when they are in the bath or shower which is explainable as water is an excellent conduit for spirit energy. Obviously in the alpha brain wave/sleep state you will hear your loved ones a lot easier too.

You may feel your face, hair or hands being stroked or touched. Always remember as well that if you ever walk through a spirit energy, it feels like cobwebs - this also includes ectoplasmic mist. So, check if there are any cobwebs first when this happens! They also love to move their own things, perhaps an ornament you have kept of theirs or a photograph. You may also get the same picture or mirror being moved so it appears haphazard or lop-sided. It is another way to get your attention.

Most Spirit people can blend easily with electrical items. I have experienced the kettle being switched on repeatedly, the doorbell ringing, microwave dinging, lights flashing on and then all going off and lights that have no dimmer switch dimming and then blazing. The best one was when I used to turn all the lights off and go up to bed. I would see a glow from my landing, go downstairs and all the lights were on again! That is a particular favourite of my dad. He also loves to put the TV on at night. It can get quite annoying. It started one November and happened to my lounge TV set every night thereafter. He then upped the ante and turned the one on in my bedroom. Some nights both would get switched on at the same time. I clearly wasn't getting the message! One night when the TVs turned on a TikTok video started playing on my phone. *Oh no,* I thought. *He wants me to go on TikTok.* The day I did my first video on TikTok in the February, the TV shenanigans stopped! Three months I had been forced to put up with it.

The phone ringing with white noise on the line is also very common. I have received many reports of people who have buried mobile phones with their loved ones and then their phone has rung and their spirit loved one's name has flashed up. I have also had the curious report of a widowed lady who was getting emails from her husband! I was very sceptical but couldn't believe my eyes when I saw the emails for myself months after he had passed. Yes, someone could have hacked into his account but in the emails were special things mentioned that only her husband would have known.

Robins or any birds visiting that remain longer than usual in the garden watching you is also quite common. They can follow you wherever you are. I've had many robins follow me as I have walked through a woodland. Once one came and sat in my hand! In America it seems to be the Cardinal bird that is the main visitor. Birds are hugely significant and are a messenger from your loved one. They will visit on the dot every day or turn up on anniversaries, perhaps even ending up in your house!

I had the most unusual situation at a client's home where she kept getting a black bird in her house. I checked every single possible way that the blackbird could get in but found nowhere he could affect entry. It wasn't until I linked up and spoke with her mum that I discovered the amazing truth. Her mum said that her daughter used to tell her all the time that she hated blackbirds, so she was sending them as a joke so she would know they were from her!

You may hear large bangs and taps that are unexplainable. My mum is a lover of huge smashes in the kitchen. I run in expecting a catastrophe and everything is sitting in place with nothing to explain the massive crash that had made us all jump!

This brings me onto another important thing to notice. Your pets are completely open to psychic phenomena, just as babies and young children are. So, if your pets are barking or looking into thin air with interest, it most probably is one of your lot visiting. I ask them to come and sit next to me. I then watch Teddy or Mia, my fur-babies, follow the spirit energy until it stops right next to me.

If your children say they have seen grandma, know that they are more than likely telling the truth. I have worried parents regularly contacting me as their young child has identified someone in a picture that visits them who died before they were even born. Your loved ones will use children to send a message. It is totally safe just as long as they aren't keeping your children awake with their enthusiasm to make contact!

One of the strongest signs I receive is through music. My dad can play his favourite song, *Bridge Over Troubled Water,* wherever I go - in a restaurant, on the radio, in a shop, all on the same day, if he is visiting. The most jaw dropping one was when I was in Thailand. I had just finished browsing in a market in Phuket and had walked into a restaurant. The first song was *Daddy's Home,* then *Bridge Over Troubled Water,* not exactly the most obvious song for Thailand. The same thing also happened in Antigua. I think he was just letting me know he had come on holiday with me! On a relevant day, or if I need him, I will just hear it again and again, so I know that he is with me. On my thirtieth birthday I was on a diving holiday in Egypt. When I walked into the hotel room, my iPod came to life and played *Bridge Over Troubled Water* and then just stopped. Listen out for the songs, it will be them reaching out!

They also, considering we are mentioning holidays, love to come away with us. They laugh when they come through and say that they can travel for free as a spirit! I once even had a spirit mum tell me the door number and the name of the hotel on her daughter's honeymoon. Be vigilant on holiday, they will send you signs. You are happy and relaxed, which is a perfect energy to be in to receive spirit messages. My mum adored owls and every time I am away I either see owls everywhere or bumble bees, her spirit animal.

People always ask me why they get more visitation in a sleep state or just drifting off. Our minds are resting, we are in a state of meditation - the alpha brain wave state, where we are completely stress free and relaxed. This is where our high vibration loved ones can blend with our quiet and still minds, contacting us or bringing messages. They can enter our dreams and visit us that way. You will know the difference as the dreams will be lucid and real. You will also remember them easily. Make sure to note every single thing you saw; every colour, the place you were and what was said, as they will all have some significance. They normally either tell us something we need to hear or are just there to give us a hug, so keep a pad at the side of the bed and write down everything as soon as you wake. If there are symbols shown that you don't understand, try visiting a dream analysis website to help decipher them.

If you see any random animals in your dream and they aren't a favourite of yours or a loved one, Google 'Spirit animal totem' as there will be a message from that animal. Spirit people are exceptionally clever. They know that by showing colours, symbols and animals, it is a short cut to getting a long message to you.

This raises an important point. Sometimes our loved ones don't just visit to say hello. I have heard thousands of stories to match my own experiences of receiving a visitation to warn me of something or to show me a way forward. My nan visited to reveal a new drug I needed to use after my road accident. My dad warned me of a new person in my life that was not very nice. I have lots of these kinds of visitations. I have also been sent emails of people's lives being saved from spirit visitation warnings. When you have a dream, as well as noting the details, always spend some time seeing how it felt. Was it nice and relaxing or did you feel a need to heed a warning?

Sleep state is most definitely the easiest way for them to blend with us as our ego doesn't get in the way of the connection. Spirit people have worked very hard to understand our atmosphere and will continually find ways to show themselves. Of course, you can also consciously go up to meet them at their frequency through meditation, if you feel the need. Meditation is the same brain frequency as sleep state. If you want to instigate the union with your loved ones, think about doing guided meditations. I have produced lots of these specifically for this purpose. There is nothing spooky or dangerous about it, so don't panic. With practice, you can go up and have full blown conversations with your loved ones, you don't need a Medium to do that for you. Give it a go if you feel you are ready, just don't do it too early if you are grieving.

Some signs will be obvious and you will know its them because of what you have been shown. For others, you won't have a clue. Best thing to do, if you have experienced anything that you think might be a sign, is to stop, close your eyes and ask in your mind, 'Who has just sent me that?' or 'Who is with me now?' TRUST your intuition and have faith that the first person you feel or see in your mind's eye is the one with you. It is that simple.

Be careful what you wish for, though. So many times I have encountered people saying they are just desperate for a sign from their loved one. When they get it, it scares the pants off them!

This has just brought to mind an intimate evening that I was doing around someone's house. The man who came through had a great sense of humour and was also very cheeky!

I said to him, 'Well, if you are so clever, do something now as your family are desperate for a sign!'

The stereo then turned itself on and a Frank Sinatra song was playing. All of the people jumped up in shock and some ran out of the house squealing with a mixture of delight and fear. The song playing was his all-time favourite and was played at his funeral. I simply love physical phenomena! It makes me tingle with delight when they do something that cannot be explained.

Another time a young lady was asking at her reading for her mum to send a clear sign. I had established that she had a wind chime in her bedroom.

I said to her mum, 'Can you move the wind chime for your daughter. If not, do something else so that she knows it is you.'

The girl was so excited when she left. At 3am (yes that is the common time for spirit visitation, presumably because it is an angel number!) her windchimes started to tinkle and it scared the crap out of her! She phoned me asking if her mum could stop doing it. Sometimes you just can't win!

So, the long and short of it is......

Stay focused - is the event that has happened explainable? If not, who might it be? Take a few seconds, as I said, still your mind after you have had an encounter and ask who is there and trust me, the first person that comes into your mind will be the person who is visiting. The more you do this the more clearly you will know who is visiting. Remember their individual signs and you will start to learn who has popped in!

Above all, I implore you to welcome your spirit visitors. They know that you love them. They know that you miss them, that is why they come to see you. Embrace their presence, acknowledge it and their efforts verbally. By doing this you will feel loved, supported and will never feel that you are alone again!

If you feel happy with their visitation, you can always go on to the next step. You can ask for interaction. You could perhaps leave a device recording and see if you get any EVP (Electronic Voice Phenomena). This is where the spirit can manipulate the ether to create sound. Hearing spirit voice phenomena still sends chills down my spine so be very sure you want to do this, as it can be terrifying to experience a discarnate voice even if it is a loved one.

One thing I must make clear is to not encourage signs and interaction with your passed loved ones when you are still grieving. You MUST grieve the physical passing of your loved one. I know that you will be desperate to know they are okay but please understand they are with you, they will be fine and they will judge when the best time is to make contact. They will assess your energy and know when it's right for them to begin a spiritual relationship with you. You can't force it to be a natural, rather than supernatural event. Also, when you are grieving, your energy is dense and heavy and they will not want to try and break into that field of grief.

There are occasions however when they will come through almost immediately. My record for bringing a spirit person through to their family is four hours after their death. My personal record is even more surprising, coming literally seconds after my ex-brother-in-law's passing. Most psychically gifted and spiritual people can get signs almost straight away as we have a tendency to reach our energy up to the Spirit World rather than focus on the physical death.

All in all, they are ready when they are ready and there is nothing that you can do to change that. More of this is explained in my next book, *What Happens When We Die?*

Next bit of sage advice is to not seek out a Medium until you have appropriately grieved. In fact, let's explore this in the next chapter...

Seeing. Mediums.

CHAPTER 22

Seeking Out a Medium

———— ★ ★ ★ ————

I know that I have already said this but please, do not go and see a Medium if you are in the most deep and rawest stages of grieving, I cannot state this clearly enough. It will do nothing but hinder your progress and could potentially damage your natural healing process. I have had to ban people from coming to see me who I knew were trying to keep their loved ones alive through me. They were still in the first stage of denial and wanted to believe that their loved one had not gone anywhere. They did not like me doing it, but I would not be responsible for delaying their grieving. Any Medium who sees a deeply bereaved client is not worth a pinch of salt, in my opinion.

Also, please go to a reputable Medium who has made it out there through word of mouth and not through pricey marketing and their own self-important BS! Just because they are on the TV does not make them an amazing Medium, trust me! Do not pay a stupid price for a reading either! There are some idiot Mediums out there who charge £250 for just thirty minutes simply because they think they are famous and amazing. The desperate ones pay it and these Mediums know it. £40 to £60 is not a bad price for an hour's reading. Anything more and you have to start asking are they more about the money rather than wanting to help you. These rip-off Mediums don't help us genuine ones. All of the sceptics and disbelievers relish in saying that we are taking money in exchange for a gift we've been given and that we are exploiting the vulnerable. Perhaps this is true of the extortionate ones.

I would like to make a few things clear to the sceptics whilst we are on the subject. People come to us for a reading, we don't force them and 'prey on the vulnerable'. We have to pay our bills and mortgage just like the next person. And as for those who say we are making money form a natural gift, you don't see them hounding actors, footballers or painters who are using their natural talent for money, do you? For them, Hollywood stars earning eight figures a movie is perfectly acceptable, but us, how dare we charge for our gift! I feel that it's a modern witch hunt and always will be, unfortunately, but we all carry on and ignore the haters! Right, that's me done on my soap box, again!

To help you get the best out of a Medium, I have written a bullet point list to make it clearer for you. By following these essential steps, you really can't go wrong.

- Firstly, ask your friends and family. A good Medium is usually found through word of mouth or reputation.
- Go to a respected site for Mediums. I always refer people to my friend's website: thespiritguides.co.uk. There are lots of Mediums listed on there, but be aware, anyone can advertise, so if you see a name that grabs you, ask people what they know about that person.
- Go to your local Spiritualist Church and watch the Mediums work. If you see one you fancy then get their details or ask the congregation who they would recommend.
- You can go to Psychic fayres as well, but again ask people for feedback after they have seen a Medium you feel drawn to.

- Be wary of those who look to under or overcharge. The going rate for half an hour to 45 minutes should be around £30 to £40 pounds. Higher profile Mediums may charge slightly more, but not extortionate money. If it is super-expensive, no matter how much they have been on the television, DO NOT pay the money! They are in it for the money and have an ego that needs preening far more than wanting to help you!
- See if the Medium is regulated by the Spiritual Workers Association or any other supporting bodies for what they are offering.
- Make sure that you are relaxed and completely open minded about the whole experience before you go. If you are stressed, depressed or have just had a bad day, Mediums will find it very hard to blend with you.
- Lots of people bring items that belong to their loved one or wear a bit of jewellery they owned, this does help the process.
- You will never be given bad news, so if they start talking about death and horror, get up and leave.
- DO NOT pay a Medium if you feel they have got nothing right. Let them know as soon as possible if it is not making sense. They should be able to gauge if you simply cannot remember the information or if the reading just isn't working.
- If they start the reading by asking you nothing but questions or let you answer with long explanations, get up and walk out.

- If you immediately don't like the energy of the Medium, excuse yourself and leave - the reading won't work.

- Do not go to a private house unless you are with a friend. Safety first. Most good Mediums will have suitable premises to work from or have such a high profile/recommendation it won't be a problem to visit their homes, but if in doubt, go with someone else.

- Don't seek out Medium after Medium if you are having a tough time. If you get a clear guided reading, go with the flow and let the angels and your loved ones help you rather than wasting your money!

- Do not leave with anything you don't understand. If the Medium has stated something that you don't understand get it clarified, or you will worry.

- Never anticipate what your loved one will say because you will create a blockage. Let them bring through what they need to, not what you want them to. I have brought the most magnificent evidence from a spirit loved one before now and the lady said, 'Oh I thought they would have mentioned my new job!' They have a limited time in the reading to get across what they want, so let them highlight what is important for you right now in that moment.

- The biggest number of emails I receive from people who get Tarot readings is about the Death Card coming up in their reading and they are worried someone is going to die! Please don't think this! The Death Card is a very positive card that usually depicts the end of a situation and new beginnings, so don't panic.

- If you are ill or under the weather, postpone the reading, the energies won't flow as well as when you are not healthy.

- Remember, don't just wish for and want one person - be open to anyone who wants to contact you and help! Inevitably they will bring who you want through next, and if you don't accept their connection, you could thwart the whole reading.

- Most of all enjoy the reading, enjoy the love brought to you and LISTEN to the advice and do something about it if you need to make a change. We can only guide you, not alter how you live your life!

- BE RESPONSIBLE. There are some desperately bad Mediums out there but thank the angels they are a minority… Just be careful!

- Don't be scared, you are not delving into anything evil or bad! Mediums are merely blending with spirit loved ones that are around you already. We do not 'conjure' or summon spirits, they come to us.

- It is not relevant what religion you are - Spirit people come through on a love vibration, not your beliefs or theirs. Religion is a manmade thing, no matter how much they didn't believe in the afterlife when they were down here because of their human faith, they will come through because they love you.

- Take a writing pad or have a friend make notes of what is said. Some Mediums will let you record the reading, some don't as it against their insurance advice.

You will no doubt come away feeling the weight of the world has slipped off your shoulders and in complete shock at what the Medium brought through. That's when you know that you have had a brilliant reading.

You have most probably seen me using the word Psychic and Medium, what's the difference? A Psychic is someone who has the ability to blend with your energy and connect with your soul and auric field. They can also project your life path, sense what is going on around you and evidence your past. They generally work with Tarot cards, runes, crystals or other divinatory tools. They work in all sorts of ways, some may want to hold your hand for the connection, whereas others may ask for an object and blend with the residual energy that's on it. This is known as psychometry. People seek out Psychics if they wish to know about their future i.e., when they are going to meet someone, are they going to move, are they going to get a new job. If you do not want any spirit contact and just want details on your life and what's going to happen, see a Psychic. I have come across some stunning Psychics who have taken my breath away about my life and my future, but ask them about a loved one in spirit, they wouldn't have a clue. Hence, not all Psychics are Mediums.

Mediums have the natural ability to connect to different layers of consciousness, where our loved ones hang out in the Spirit World (as explained in a previous chapter). So, rather than blend with your soul, their source of information is from a spirit person. They have the ability to raise their consciousness to a higher vibration (alpha/theta/sleep state) whilst awake and blend with spirit energies. They also have the ability to blend with deeper states of consciousness, channelling through their guides from the higher realms and spirit communicators in trance. Some can also blend with the angel realms as well.

Mediums use different senses to receive information from the spirit communicator:

Seeing – Clairvoyant (Translates as *Clear Seeing*)
Hearing – Clairaudient
Tasting – Clairgustance
Smelling – Clairalience
Feeling – Clairsentience
Knowing – Claircognance

Some Mediums can connect with the Spirit World by just using one of these senses where others are able to use them all. I am lucky that the Spirit World uses all of the above with me to bring their messages to my sitter. A good Medium will be able to describe your loved one, their relationship to you, the way they passed, evidence memories you shared, possibly relevant names including the communicator's, perhaps addresses and things that should convince you who you are talking to. They should be able to give irrefutable proof of life after physical death. These sorts of Mediums usually call themselves Spiritual Mediums or Evidential Mediums. The main body of their reading is spirit contact and proving the afterlife. They will bring messages to you from your loved ones but don't work with the future or what is going on around you. If you hope to hear from your loved ones who have passed over then see a Medium, a REPUTABLE one.

Psychic Mediums, like me, will be able to blend with your loved ones and secure evidence of the communicator's identity. We can also pass on messages from the spirit person that will be relevant on what's going on in your life. We have the ability to drop our energy down at will to see what is also going on in your life, along with the future and the past if it is relevant. This means that we can blend with your auric field for a while and then send our frequency back up to the Spirit World within a second.

For instance, a spirit dad may say he is very concerned about you but is unable to communicate any further information about it. So, I will drop down, blend with your auric field and find out what the concern is. I can then pop back up and blend straight back with your dad knowing what the problem is that he is highlighting. I think the best movie that shows how it all works is *Ghost!* I went and watched that movie four times in a row when it was in the cinema! Most of it is well explained but I am not sure on the groaning shadows that took the baddies away!

What you are looking for is a Medium who basically won't shut up. They just land statement after statement and you just have to say yes or no. Let us say, for instance, you receive a message stating: "I have a mum or grandmother figure here and she says that you are feeling down and wants to give you a bunch of roses." It's safe to say don't listen to the rest of the message. *Stab in the dark* comes to mind.

However, if the Medium says, "I feel I have your mum here. She passed in her sixties with a heart attack, I hear the name Joan connecting to her (and it's her name or your name or a person close to her) and she passed at 3 o'clock in the Royal Hospital in London and wants to give you your favourite yellow roses because your birthday is coming up and her passing anniversary is also…" Sit up and listen.

As I said earlier in the list, if they ask you more questions than give you statements, walk away. You should be just confirming what they have already said or making sense of an unusual vision the Medium has seen. In essence, it's the same as any service or industry, you are going to get the bad apples. It is up to you to be responsible and not be so desperate for contact with your loved one that you end up going to someone quite awful. There is no real regulatory body that can deal with the rip-offs, which is unfortunate so please be very careful.

You want this to be a magical, spiritual experience where you get comfort, closure and connection - don't ruin it out of sheer impatience. Most good Mediums have a waiting list, be prepared for your reading to not occur immediately. Normally, I have found that the people who wait have the reading come at exactly the right time in their life. It is almost like it has been orchestrated in unison with the Universe and the spirit communicator.

It is an awesome experience when you start getting unbelievable facts that no one could know from a stranger. Value it, record it and treasure it - it really is your loved one talking to you on the phone from Heaven.

How. Amazing.

CHAPTER 23

The Rise to Celebrity

———— ★ ★ ★ ————

This chapter is a little bittersweet as I really enjoyed this next phase of my journey immensely but it also proved heavy on the material side of life.

With me being all over the country doing my demonstrations, my name started to get everywhere. Radio stations all over the world began inviting me on as a guest. This inevitably led to TV companies asking for me to take part in their programmes. I didn't sit very well with the TV stuff initially, to be honest, as what I had seen of paranormal shows up until then was akin to watching a circus, especially the paranormal and ghost-hunt shows. There always had to be some drama and something terrifying the presenters. It made great TV and obviously *Most Haunted* was booming in views, proving very popular in its day, but it really wasn't my cup of tea if I'm truthful.

Along with the TV stuff came the copious requests for magazine work and writing. This is where I started to get a buzz, documenting my experiences and sharing my esoteric knowledge. Those days, which spanned from 2006 until 2012, represented me in my element. Everything I touched turned to gold. My workshops and seminars were sold out up to a year in advance. The waiting list for a personal reading was over two years and every theatre show, dem and church attendance was heaving and sold out. People were coming from other countries to have a reading with me and the pressure was immense but so exciting.

In 2009 the call came for *Angels*. I had to go to the Sky studios in London. I was so impressed as I had a chauffeur pick me up and take me for the auditions. Curiously, I had to do readings for so many people including the head of Sky Real Lives, many producers, the director and staff members of Liberty Bell Productions - who were producing the series. I had no idea what that had to do with angels, but I enjoyed every minute with all of them!

I was successful in my audition and within a couple of months I was again chauffeured to the studios to start filming. I had my own dressing room and runners, which I found very peculiar; they would literally get me anything I wanted.

When the first day came, I was in makeup and Gloria Hunniford sat down next to me and introduced herself. Despite being a national treasure, she spoke to all of us like we were having a coffee morning. I met the lovely Glennyce Eckersley, an angel expert, and Paranormal Psychologist, Chris French, who I have to say was exceptionally kind to me when he can be quite brutal to some Psychics!

The filming had to be done within a week, meaning we had to do a whole series in that time, so thank God I was focused and a natural at being filmed. Gloria even said to me when we were sitting opposite each other in the studio, 'What other series have you done; I don't think I have seen one retake yet?'

She was very surprised to hear my back-catalogue amounted to just two programmes. She had assumed I was very experienced, something I took as a huge compliment. My main aim on that first series was to pick someone out of the audience and do an angel card and psychic reading then and there, no practice, no time to link in, I just had to get on with it. I also sat in the crowd and was asked my opinion on things that were discussed about angel phenomena. It was a beautiful programme and the people I met from all over the world that wanted to share their stories of how angels saved their lives was such a humbling experience.

I felt a bit daunted when I had to do a live reading for William Roach (Ken Barlow in Coronation Street). As I sat in front of him, I saw that he was one of the most spiritual people that I had ever met. My soul recognised his immediately. The reading went on for ages, I was so disappointed that the edited version made it really short. I suppose it's understandable given each show only lasted half an hour.

Angels came out top of the ratings and to sit with my friends and family and watch the airing of the first episode was such a proud moment for me. Well, apart from my mum moaning that I kept sniffing! (It's a thing I do when working with Spirit, so shoot me!) I travelled to Scotland with Gloria for interviews promoting the show and we did a live show on *Live from Studio Five*, where I met so many celebrities who were absolutely lovely. There were of course a few divas, but they are for me to keep in my secrets box!

Following the series, I was asked to judge the quarter finals of Miss World as a celebrity judge. I also had my paranormal investigation film, *The Birdbrook Ghost Hunt*, aired at the Southend Film Festival, where I spent a thrilling evening with many celebrities, especially A-lister Ray Winstone who was an absolute joy. *The Birdbrook Ghost Hunt* is now aired on my YouTube

Channel if you fancy watching it! It turned out to be a VERY scary paranormal investigation!

I was the guest Medium on *Come Dine with Me* as I have already mentioned. Due to being slightly burned on this occasion I refused relentless requests to go on a new show at the time called *The Only Way is Essex*. Every time a new season started; I would get the phone call asking me to be on it as their Medium. I refused each time as they stated that they could not give me editing rights. I was so scared of being made to look an idiot again.

I also had a short documentary made about me, *A Sisters Loss* on Sky TV.

Inevitably I was asked to have a meeting with an agent which I supposed came with the territory. I had mixed feelings about this but I know my ego took over at the time. The man asked me to lose more weight even though I felt fab as a size 14. There were mumblings of teeth whitening, hair being died darker and elocution lessons as I sounded too common. In fact, once he likened me to a holiday camp performer as I was far too friendly with the audience. Despite this, (and I so want to punch myself right now for writing this!) I was seeing bright lights and me being able to reach the world even easier. The icing on the cake was he was also the agent for the late Colin Fry. The day I walked in and sat having a cup of tea with Colin will never leave me. I had watched him for years on the TV and now he was asking me if he could be my management, I agreed.

After a few months I was delighted to learn that a second series of Angels had been commissioned and that I was to have half the show. I was so elated, what an absolute honour and a compliment! I couldn't wait to start filming again. It was such a respectful programme and the fan mail I got made me so emotional as they were so heartfelt. One was from a gentleman who had lost his wife and was distraught. He said that his daughter would come over and watch Angels on a Friday night with him and that it gave him so much comfort that his wife was with the angels. He thanked me for giving him a reason to look forward to something again.

TV is a very powerful thing. I had publishers asking me to write books and literally was hounded every day by media and the public. I ended up employing people to help set up shows and organise events. Richard, my brother, had a huge part in this, as well as my sister Sarah selling merchandise. It was a wonderful time and we had the greatest laughs as we travelled around the country.

The day I sat in a dressing room applying makeup, wearing a handmade ball gown waiting to go on after Colin Fry, was when I knew I had achieved exactly what I wanted. I walked out onto the stage facing three thousand people and nailed one reading after another. I had done it; I had reached the top. After the show Colin and I sat and I signed his books for the fans. I knew then that I wanted to be the person sitting there with my own book that people wanted to sign. The world was my oyster and there was nothing going to stop me, or was there?

It felt good to feel wanted and to be so popular. I don't think I ever had a night out without someone recognising me and wanting to say hello, ask me a question or take a picture. This was especially so when I met Brian Belo, the winner of the TV show *Big Brother* at a Polo event. We got on really well and would hit Nando's, as celebs do, and both of us would relish the attention we got at *Bas Vegas*. (Basildon Leisure Park in Essex).

I was asked to celebrity social gatherings and had many celebrity clients who came from all over the country to see me. It was quite weird to begin with, having famous people sitting in my conservatory having a reading. I treated them just as I did any other person, to be honest. To me, I had a duty to the Spirit World to deliver, the person in front of me held no relevance in their social standing. It was also quite peculiar when famous spirit people came through, I had to try and contain my excitement and remain professional.

What I did notice with celebrities were a lot of them were definitely young souls. Not all (I wouldn't want to tar everyone with the same brush), but the vast majority were. I have mentioned previously about old souls who normally choose incarnations that have tougher challenges and more in-depth human experiences. They do not care for the material world and have no passion for money, fame and status. Whereas new souls seem to crave material things and gauge money and status as their means to happiness. They don't have much of a hard life and normally their main downfalls are themselves, through their inner-demons - a lack of self-worth, addictions, desires to be in the limelight and their passion for notoriety. Young souls are the robbers that win the lottery or those who inherit millions and become a socialite. They have no wish for hard human experiences until their soul cluster matures. It used to make me smile when they would attend a session totally stressed and at exploding point just because they weren't sure if their agent was representing them properly! Oh, to just have that as a main problem in life!

I always tried to keep grounded during this time being around the glitz and glamour. The first TV documentary, *Desolate*

Landscape (as mentioned in Chapter Ten), got me ready for being in front of the camera and working with a crew. I am a natural to be honest, I have no qualms about public speaking or being in front of a camera. When I am bringing spirit through or teaching and doing social media on TikTok and YouTube everything just flows. However, if you had me on stage talking about something not related to the paranormal, I would be horrendous no doubt!

I don't think it would be fair to comment on all of the different documentaries and programmes I did as some were amazing experiences whereas others weren't all that great. I had so many offers but most of them I felt didn't hold integrity to Mediumship and the afterlife so I would always politely decline them.

I did attend one meeting for a new show that was to be aired. I met with the Executive Producers in an office in West London. I sat with my mouth gaping and couldn't believe what I was hearing. One of the producers made his first mistake by calling me 'sweetheart' in a rather derogatory way. He kept pronouncing it as 'sweedart'. He made me cringe. The show was basically me taking people to well known 'evil' haunted locations and putting them into coffins and seeing how long they could last after I had summoned demons or evil spirits. The winner would win a huge cash prize.

What the holy fuck?

I spouted out a very principled view of what I thought before standing up rather abruptly and flouncing across the room, in an effort to portray my contempt at such a preposterous idea. The mistake I made is that, upon offering a last rebellious look back, I opened the door only to find myself marching into a cupboard! After placing the broom back in its place, I cleared my throat and located the actual exit. Oh, how we laughed at that one.

The second series of *Angels* was incredible. My half of the show was known as the *Street Angel*. We travelled all over the country and I had to ask strangers if they wanted an angel card reading. It was such a lovely experience travelling with the crew and runners, who were an absolute joy. I really did feel like royalty! I was also asked to do a live reading for Melinda Messenger on a Christmas special at the *Live from Studio Five* studios. I had to haul back to London to do the reading and what a pleasure that lady is. She was so friendly, sincere and so kind. Yep, along with Ray she is one of my favourite celebrities!

I then continued to be invited to celeb parties, small get-togethers at their homes, polo celebrity matches, and (sorry but I have to say it) Paul Young - one of my favourite singers from the eighties - was a joy! I was seeing what it was like to enjoy the finer things in life. I didn't have to worry about money and loved being in the public eye. I lived in my ego and not in my soul and that's where everything started to go wrong.

The. Fall.

CHAPTER 24

The Fall from Celebrity

———— ★ ★ ★ ————

Working with Colin Fry naturally led to me working alongside the late Derek Acorah, Steve Holbrook and many other well-established Mediums. Steve always made me feel so welcome, he is a super guy. I had reached the dizziest heights that any Medium could wish for. I was at the top of my industry and couldn't have felt happier.

A couple of things were starting to pinch though. I was hearing from someone that a very well-known Medium was booking the same venue or area a week before me to try and thwart my shows. It never did but the fact this was happening started to dig away at my insecurities. Why would people want to be so hurtful? Why did they not embrace me as another fellow worker?

The numbers game was also starting to weigh heavily on my shoulders. I found that I was worrying about bums on seats in theatres to cover the six staff I now employed. I felt like I was turning into a money-making machine to cover venue fees, insurances, advertising, vehicles, equipment, staff and wages. To be honest, it started to become a bit of a slog and I now realise I began to lose myself in the world of commerce and materialism. I didn't feel like a Medium anymore, I felt like a commodity chugging out one dead person after another. I started to feel quite lonely.

The Spirit people were always ready and willing to jump in to speak to their loved ones en masse, so the messages got harder to contain and keep in order. The stress was hitting me hard and I came to realise I didn't know who my friends were anymore. I had so many people around me but was it because of who I was? That's all I could think about, day-in day-out. A small demon within me used to tell me regularly that if I didn't have this gift no one would be interested in me at all. I wasn't myself and started to allow my old feelings of insecurity in. By 2010 I was by no means the greatest version of myself.

The decline started on my 40th birthday. I had run myself ragged and had developed bronchitis and a throat infection. I couldn't talk and knew that I had to travel up to Birmingham, to do a show with Colin at the Alexandra Theatre. This was also on my 40th birthday so I would be driving up with a temperature, being unable to speak or work properly then drive back that night to Essex which would have taken six hours on top of doing the show. My family had arranged a huge birthday celebration for me and so I had to get back for that the following day. They were exceptionally concerned about how ill I was and threatened to hide my keys. For the first time in a very long time, I valued my health rather than work. I could sit and smile with my family on my birthday but not drive for six hours and address a 5,000 strong crowd when I couldn't even talk. I ended up cancelling the show and it didn't go down too well. That ended my work with Colin. I didn't even get a goodbye and thank you (more like a fuck you) from the agent. My confidence dropped drastically and I questioned myself repeatedly as to whether I should have put my health or work first. How bad is that?

I met a man and started to date him out of sheer loneliness. He was manipulative and toxic and drove me apart from my family. I wasn't happy and started to fade away within myself, popping out when needed as *The Amazing Nicky Alan*. I was exhausted; it was nonstop and I didn't know how to say no.

I decided to go away for Christmas 2011 and New Year to Florida as I adore Disney, especially Tinkerbell. I needed to escape and rest up for a while. I loved that holiday apart from being with my dickhead partner who was quite happy to spend my money and go for free. I never thought to question it I just needed someone with me.

Feeling refreshed, we returned and I had a new spring in my step. There was a plan for a tour in Australia and America. I had also been approached by the Discovery Channel with a possible programme that would take me around the world. I had a view of getting my first book finished and wanted to put the whole of the last two years behind me. I made a vow that I would also cut down on my work and spend more time with my real friends and family.

Friends, you certainly find out who your friends are when you disappear into an abyss of misery and darkness through no fault of your own.

On 23 January 2012, two weeks after Disney, I woke up with a cold sweat having had the worst nightmare. I dreamt that I had been hit by an invisible force and realised it was a car smash. Not knowing when and where, I put it down to a bad dream and left to go to Devon. I was in the process of buying a holiday home down there as I had fallen in love with Torbay the first time I had gone there working in the Riviera Centre with Colin and Derek.

Dickhead was driving as we turned to pull into a pub in Devon for some dinner. I heard the screeching tyres as the car came careering towards me. I couldn't move as the seatbelt wouldn't undo. The sickening thud as the two cars connected secured the end of my life as I knew it.

That young girl will never know how she changed my life due to her error in driving. I became bedbound in agonising pain with unexplained exhaustion. A year later after copious amounts of hospital tests I was diagnosed with a brain trauma injury that led to the severe end of ME (chronic fatigue syndrome) and Fibromyalgia. Dickhead knew I had a long-term prognosis of chronic illness, so helped himself to my credit cards and left without a trace.

With each cancellation of a show or a reading, a part of my soul died with it. My faith was lost to a cloud of bereavement, hate, anger and fear. One day a regular celebrity client phoned me asking for a reading. I explained I was seriously ill, she put the phone down before I even finished my sentence. I was done. I was no longer any use to anyone.

Banks don't care if you have had an accident so as I lay in bed year after year I said goodbye to my home in Essex, my holiday home in Devon and ended up homeless for eight months. I was in debt up to my eyeballs thanks to dickhead and had nothing but my two little rescue dogs to keep me going. The magazine work dried up, the offers from the media disappeared and I was the old newspaper fluttering in the wind from the day before.

Nicky Alan was a name that now had an attachment, 'wasn't that the old Medium who was brilliant, where is she now?'

The dizzying heights that I had reached through blood sweat and tears had been lost. I had once seen myself as a shining star, bright and bold shining light into every crevice of a dark velvet sky. As I descended into the death of my old self, I only saw a star for what it really was, an explosion of life that once was. The fall was every bit as painful with each year that went by, my prognosis by the medical profession, nothing would ever change.

I do look back now and then and think, 'What if? Where would I be now? Would I be touring the world bringing love, peace and proof of the afterlife? Would I have my tenth bestseller racing through the literary charts? Would I be a household name as one of the world's best Mediums? The answer is yes, most probably.

This story is pretty much a prequel to my first book, *M.E Myself and I: Diary of a Psychic*. My journey ends in this book at the most destructive and yet, in many respects, the most magnificent part of my life. After the devastation, once again, the Spirit World and Angel Realms grabbed the reins of my existence and changed me into who I am today, minus the bright lights.

All I can offer now due to my condition is teaching on social media, the odd Zoom Evening of Mediumship, online courses and meditations and my writing. It is too exhausting to do individual readings for people now. I could probably manage to do a TV show, but I am not exactly out there being able to advertise the fact! It breaks my heart, as every single day I gets tens of people asking for a private reading and I have to explain that I simply cannot afford the energy that it takes to devote one hour to just one person. It frustrates me as I have so much knowledge and so much proof of the afterlife to give the world. I have no idea why I haven't healed one hundred per cent. Perhaps they wanted me to teach the world through my books. I have to admit though I bloody miss the theatre evenings, the spiritualist churches, the town halls and the wonderful people in them, just as I miss working as a Major Investigation Detective.

However, the angels and my spirit loved ones always say to me, 'Never live in your past as it never will serve your future.'

I wouldn't be here writing this now if it wasn't for them forever pushing me on.

Absolute. Legends.

CHAPTER 25

What My Bosses Taught Me

———— ★ ★ ★ ————

I have to admit that I never thought for a million years I would end up being a full time Psychic Medium, social media influencer and an author. I was completely set on being a Detective for the whole of my life, followed by retirement in a hot country and general pottering about. But life doesn't happen like we plan, does it? Yes, I knew that I had come from a magical ancestry but to me it was like breathing, completely natural and not to be shared - certainly not as a career! But when I started to see how I transformed people's lives and how they reacted to my ability when communicating with the Spirit World, I became awake. Spirit contact and proving the afterlife ran like fire through my blood. I couldn't stop it, even if I had tried. The only way for it to be sated was to do readings for people and help them understand that we are eternal.

There is nothing on this earth worse than losing a loved one and then thinking that it's all over. With my passion to help as an empath and my spiritual abilities, I know that I will not halt in bringing the celestial planes to the people until I take my last physical breath. Well, to be fair, no doubt I will be doing something very similar in my next life, if we can keep the planet going for long enough!

The journey that the Spirit World took me on from haunting me with a screaming spirit baby to now has been nothing short of miraculous. Each spirit person that has come to me has always brought something new to the table, whether it's a new symbol a different way to prove their existence, or how they can bring smell and taste to my senses. They are relentless in trying to get through to their loved ones, I just wish that the whole of mankind knew this! People go through so much torment, loneliness and pain when they have a bereavement. Those that have no clue their loved one is sitting right next to them are the type I want to reach. That's where I step in and try to get them to realise there is no death of the soul.

My life, I believe, would have been so much different if I had been a Police Officer for thirty years. It also wouldn't have been the same without having the road accident. I would not have appreciated the planet. I would not have had time to meditate and explore the Spirit World and the Angel Realms. I certainly wouldn't have reached people in their millions with my teachings and ability through the internet. I have been able to touch people all over the world with my knowledge and messages of hope, something which makes me feel so humble. I live almost as a hybrid - half on the earth, half in the Spirit World - knowing that I am never alone.

My bosses have taught me to forgive myself and others in my life, to let go of materialism, to make our incarnations down here based on happiness and love and not how big your house is or how fat your bank account is. They have taught me humility, compassion and unconditional love, always. I just don't know what I would do without them, except that undoubtedly the Spirit World has made me a better person. I feel more balanced, emotionally complete and tranquil within. I also now know that abundance rests on how happy I am and how much I am loved rather than what I have achieved each day. I no longer people-please and have learned to love myself unconditionally, all aided by guides and spirit loved ones.

I just want to share this with you. In the last week my fragile ego has taken over a bit and made me feel that all of the work I have put into this book will go unnoticed, that no one will want to read it. I have almost been convincing myself that the time spent on it has just been a hobby and will be left on this laptop just for me to peruse on occasion. My mum and dad must have heard my thoughts and misgivings because my beautiful psychic friend, Anna, who always comes at the right time messaged me yesterday. Among other things that were so spot on, she said that my mum had told her, 'People DO want to hear what you have to say. Please keep going with the book!'

I was so amazed to read this as Anna lives back in Essex and we stay connected now and then through social media but she had no idea of my fears about the book. In one fell swoop her contact eradicated my worries and has spurred me on to finish this and share it with the world. We all benefit from messages from Mediums, even if we have the ability to link up to the Spirit World ourselves! So, Mum, I am going to send this book out and hope that it touches the souls of those who need it.

I truly hope that those who come across this book get some form of comfort, along with the knowledge that we never ever die, we just move on. Whilst your loved ones are waiting for you, I and all the other beautiful Mediums out there will bridge the gap until you meet them again one fine and fateful day. X

God. Bless.

Biography

———— ★ ★ ★ ————

Nicky is a born Psychic Medium coming from many generations of gifted Psychics before her. She officially started her psychic work 31 years ago. For eighteen years she was a police officer ending as a Major Investigation bereavement trained Detective in Essex Police. Following medical retirement in 2003 and by public demand she has achieved a very high profile in the spiritual industry as a full time Psychic Medium, Spiritual Teacher, Writer and Angel Expert.

Since 2003, she has been a freelance paranormal writer regularly published in mainstream spiritual magazines including Chat its Fate, Psychic News, Psychic Vision, Kindred Spirit, Paranormal News and Spirit and Destiny. She is the current columnist in Take a Break's Fate & Fortune Magazine as The Psychic Detective. She is also a resident features writer in Haunted Magazine.

She is the current columnist in Take a Break's Fate & Fortune Magazine as The Psychic Detective, UK and Australia. She is also a resident features writer in the international Haunted Magazine.

Nicky's debut spiritual memoir, *M.E Myself and I: Diary of a Psychic* was a Number One Amazon hit as the hottest new release in her genre.

She is noted for her international appearances on radio (winner best Show/guest for 'Angels' *Haunted Devon FM*) tours with the late Colin Fry and TV programmes including *Street Seer* Gifted channel, *A Sister's Loss*, Sky One, *Live from Studio Five* channel 5 (with Melinda Messenger, Ian Wright and Kate Walsh) *Come Dine with Me* (guest Medium) *Angels* (two seasons with Gloria Hunniford, Glennyce Eckersley and Chris French) and cinema film paranormal documentary *The Birdbrook Ghost Hunt*.

She has carried out European theatre tours, seminars, retreats and workshops to 3,000 strong crowds on the afterlife and angel phenomena resulting in a high social media platform.

She has produced many guided meditations and has a successful online spiritual living course *Prism Living*. She also helps the public through her spiritual education videos as *The Bedroom Guru* on YouTube and Nicky_alan_psychic on TikTok.

Since her catastrophic road accident in 2012 limiting her touring, she is now pursuing her passion as a Spiritual Author and teacher. Aside from writing she has a passion for the sea and adores walking her two dogs Teddy and Mia on the beaches of Devon where she now lives.

Where to find Nicky

————— ★ ★ ★ —————

Thank you for purchasing *The Rise and Fall of Britain's Best Psychic Medium*. My sincere hope is that you have derived as much pleasure from reading this book as I have in creating it. If you have a few moments, please feel free to add your review of the book at your favourite online site for feedback, it really will help!

Also, please visit my website for news on upcoming works and events at http://www.nickyalan.co.uk

You can also connect with me on: Amazon: https://www.amazon.co.uk/Nicky-Alan/e/B08LDNS64D/ref=aufs_dp_fta_dsk

Twitter: http://twitter.com/@nickyalan07

Instagram: Nicky Alan (@nickyalan333) • Instagram photos and videos

Facebook: https://www.facebook.com/nicky.alan.355

Or why not come along and watch my helpful Spiritual Education videos on my YouTube Channel (9) Nicky Alan - The Bedroom Guru - YouTube

TikTok: https://www.tiktok.com/@nicky_alan_psychic?_t=8X1OJCLgoKc&_r=1

Thank you once again for sharing my journey,

May the angels bless you always, Nicky x

Other Books by Nicky Alan

――――― ★ ★ ★ ―――――

M.E Myself and I: Diary of a Psychic

This is a brutally honest story of a woman struck down with M.E and Fibromyalgia in the prime of her life as a successful TV Psychic Medium. Left with nothing but two dustbin bags, demons from the past and her two dogs, she embarks on an incredible journey. Grieving her old life and begrudgingly accepting guidance from angels and spirit guides after losing her faith, she finds a reason to live from the brink of suicide by experiencing celestial miracles and a passion to write. This inspirational self-help spiritual memoir highlights a chronic illness pandemic sweeping through the world that society has shamefully neglected. Her esoteric voice representing the 'millions missing' brings hope, faith and a definitive strength of the human spirit during the injustice of one life altering episode after another.

What people are saying about this book:

Speaking from her heart, Nicky reaches out to each one of us with compassion and love as she openly and honestly shares her most intimate life details through such an amazing course of events and synchronicities. This book is a refreshing and real story. Horrific, but real. Her sufferings have made her the strong, compassionate woman she now is, a shining light, a beacon of hope to the world. This is her unique contribution to humanity, timeless in its strong message of hope to us all. You will not be able to put this book down, guaranteed!

– Eileen McCourt - Spiritual Author and Teacher

An autobiography that will take you on a journey of tears, inspiration and hope. I could not put this book down, it's so much more than a dairy of Nicky's life. If you are going through a tough time or a bereavement this book will help you get through the dark days and give you comfort in knowing your loved ones are always by your side. I always thought a gifted psychic would have a rosy life with 24-hour communication to those upstairs! Well, how wrong was I!

At times I found it shocking to learn what Nikki has gone through. From a tough childhood, bereavement, bankruptcy and a debilitating illness she is still standing, remains positive and has utter faith that this is her journey. This book made me realise the angels and spirit guides are always by your side, you just have to call them in.

A corker of a book and one I will pick up again when I am having a tough time!

– Annie Conlon - TV Producer

Have you ever read a book and felt like you were being drawn into its pages? That it captivated you so much that you couldn't put it down? Well, this is how I felt after reading Nicky's book. I read it in around 6 hours, it had me hooked. I did have to annoyingly stop to make lunch, but then I was straight back to it. If I was living alone, I would've just grabbed a banana and carried on reading! I could relate to a lot of what she was saying, that after I read it, I felt like we were old friends. Even though we've never met.

Nicky writes with such deep, heartfelt and honest raw emotion, as so many harrowing and horrific life changing events are thrown at her, one after the other. Her courage, inner strength and resolve shine so brightly throughout this book. Triumph over adversity - way more than anyone could possibly bear - but Nicky does time and time again. A true story that brings inspiration and hope, and shows that with real gutsy determination, faith, trust and spirit, you really can turn your life around. I can't recommend this book highly enough. Enjoy!

– Suzanne Clark

I only got the book yesterday and cannot put it down. Nicky Alan is an inspiration to anyone who is suffering not only from ME but unseen illnesses. She truly opens your eyes to the spiritual world and that angels are always with us. To go through so much and come out the other side is a miracle but to also write books, is truly amazing.

– Francesca Irvine

Paperback and Kindle version are available at Amazon:

https://www.amazon.co.uk/M-Myself-Psychic-Miracle-Surviving/dp/1789044510/ref=cm_cr_arp_d_pdt_img_top?ie=UTF8

Audio and signed copies are available at my website:

https://www.nickyalan.co.uk/product/m-e-myself-and-i-diary-of-a-psychic-signed/

https://www.nickyalan.co.uk/product/m-e-myself-and-i-audiobook/

New Release from Nicky Coming Soon!

---★ ★ ★---

What Happens When We Die?

This book is a compellingly unique guide to what happens to our soul when we die and provides the most intricate detail of Heaven with all of its layers of existence. Nicky takes us on an incredible soul ride from physical death right through to our next reincarnation. With her esoteric knowledge and ability to connect to the Spirit World, Spirit Guides and Angel Realms, she answers every single thing that you would want to know about the afterlife. With real life spirit contact stories, hospice nurse anecdotes and true Near Death Experiences even the hardened sceptic may have to rethink is death really the final ending?

Printed in Great Britain
by Amazon